The
Green
Witch's
GARDEN
JOURNAL

FROM HERBS AND FLOWERS TO
MUSHROOMS AND VEGETABLES,
*Your Planner and Logbook
for a Magical Garden*

ARIN MURPHY-HISCOCK
AUTHOR OF **The Green Witch**

ADAMS MEDIA
NEW YORK   LONDON   TORONTO   SYDNEY   NEW DELHI

Adams Media
An Imprint of Simon & Schuster, Inc.
100 Technology Center Drive
Stoughton, Massachusetts 02072

First Adams Media hardcover edition March 2023

ADAMS MEDIA and colophon are trademarks of Simon & Schuster.

For information about special discounts for bulk purchases, please contact Simon & Schuster Special Sales at 1-866-506-1949 or business@simonandschuster.com.

The Simon & Schuster Speakers Bureau can bring authors to your live event. For more information or to book an event contact the Simon & Schuster Speakers Bureau at 1-866-248-3049 or visit our website at www.simonspeakers.com.

Interior design by Colleen Cunningham
Illustrations by Sara Richard
Interior images © 123RF/Eleonora Konnova, Irina Vaneeva, Christos Georghiou; Getty Images/eyewave, tigerstrawberry, Maksim-Manekin, littleclie, CSA-Printstock, kenny371

Manufactured in China

10 9 8 7 6 5 4 3 2 1

ISBN 978-1-5072-2006-1

Contains material adapted from the following title published by Adams Media, an Imprint of Simon & Schuster, Inc.: *The Green Witch's Garden* by Arin Murphy-Hiscock, copyright © 2021, ISBN 978-1-5072-1587-6.

Contents

Introduction

TENDING A GARDEN GIVES YOU a deep, rich, and personal connection to the earth. As a green witch, you work closely with nature through your garden, and keeping various records is an important part of tracking growth, challenges, and successes. Referencing those records can be a supportive, affirming practice, and inspire new ideas and directions for your magical gardening.

Having a garden is an ideal way for a green witch to not only curate plants for magical work and form a connection with those plants, but also connect to the energy of them at different points in their life cycles. Keeping track of your garden in a mundane—as well as magical—sense is key to that connection process in the first year of your garden and the many years to come. With the help of *The Green Witch's Garden Journal* you will be able to note important gardening details, such as plant descriptions, planting histories, blooming and harvesting notes, as well as the spells and magical associations you use your plants for. Then in future years, you can use this information to better both your garden and its harvest *and* your magical work.

This journal is also an investment in your garden's well-being. Writing down when you started seeds indoors and when you moved the seedlings outside to harden helps you be consistent and plan ahead appropriately. For example, did a particular variety of cherry tomato just not produce the harvest you hoped for? Consult your records before you buy seeds the next year to make sure you're not buying that same disappointing variety again. You can also keep track of the weather and how it affected your plants' energies. How did that overabundance of water at the midpoint of your peak growing season affect your plants? Was it an oddly early fall? When was the last hard frost? You can also note the astrological and lunar information associated with the times you planted and harvested and see if that affected your garden's output or health.

Finally, you'll want to write a blessing for your garden journal. Consecrate it to the use of your garden, your journey along the path of green witchcraft, and the good of nature at large. Here's one to use as inspiration:

Book, be for me a journal
Of life in my garden.
Be the connection between our past together, our fruitful present,
and our coming future.

Book, be for me a grimoire
Of garden magics and spiritual celebration.
May my garden and I continue to grow in harmony together.

Nature, bless this book with love and joy,
With knowledge and insight.
Help me to remain attuned to the energy of life
That flows in and around my garden.

Garden journal, plant grimoire,
I name you blessed,
In the name of the sun, the soil, the rain, and the breeze.

So may it be.
It is so.

Whether your garden is indoors, outdoors, on a balcony, in a window box, or on a windowsill, it is a spiritual gateway to a rewarding connection with nature. Celebrate that connection by using *The Green Witch's Garden Journal* to craft a gardening journal that honors your work, and rejoice in the many blessings your garden brings.

How to Use This Book

THE ART OF GARDENING IS part magic and part science, part practical and part instinctual. This book will serve as a pragmatic, but important tool in your magical garden. Designed to be easy-to-use and flexible, this journal will help you track your garden throughout the first season, and then year after year.

Section One

Every endeavor starts with a plan and the first section in this journal will help you do just that, by showing you how to plan a garden space to meet both your magical and practical needs. You'll evaluate things like the average level of rainfall in your area, the amount of sunlight, when the ground gets cold and freezes, and what the specific soil conditions and climate are like in your garden. Items like these may seem a bit tedious to observe and record but they are critical for you to get in touch with your growing environment and make a connection to the earth around you so you can properly work with it to enhance your garden.

You'll also consider what type of garden you'll want to fulfill your magical goals. Do you want an astrological garden, a moon garden, or perhaps one centered around the elements? You'll find descriptions of each of these in Section 1, as well as ideas for garden design, hardscape, and other elements that will help align your garden with your higher purpose. Please note that one thing you won't find in this journal are plant recommendations—for those, you should turn to the comprehensive lists of magical plants and their uses in *The Green Witch's Garden*.

Section Two

Once you've planned and planted your garden, this journal will become your diary and gardening friend throughout the season. While it may seem like extra work after an afternoon of gardening to sit down and record your journal entries, you won't regret it. Keeping a record of the lives of your plants (their germination schedules, blooming times, harvest times, and so on) not only keeps you in touch with those plants and how to best nurture them; it also gives you the tools to anticipate the needs of future plants in your garden.

The heart of this journal is the weekly entries, one for each week of the year. You should set aside time each week you're gardening to sit down with your journal and record what happened. The journal entries are designed to allow you to create a comprehensive record of each week. You can record:

- Rainfall totals
- Average temperatures
- Moon phases
- Astrological information
- Pests and weeds
- Your fertilizer schedule
- Pruning
- Any wildlife you observed
- General daily notes
- Harvesting

Use these fields however you want, but the more detailed your notes, the more useful your journal! Year after year, it's easy to forget the details of any season, but you might find in future years that a great way to pass some time is to sit and read your old journals to see how your growing space transforms and flourishes, and reflect on the progress you've made as a gardener.

This section will help you keep running notes over the course of the weeks as you garden. In this log, you can make notations on the weather, garden visitors, seasons, tasks, and so on. This section is strictly focused on the plants' practical growing information, as your plants' magical uses and associations will be recorded in Section 3.

Section Three

This portion of the book is a reference section with a magical touch. Material from Section 2 can feed into these pages. For example, you can record preferences for each of your plants, germination information and dates, blooming and harvest dates and times, and any special notes. However, this is also where you can document things like the magical associations for your plants, what spells you plan on using them for, what magical qualities you hope to see in them, and how your plants grew and flourished under your care. Each template has an area where you can draw the plant, paste images or pressed leaves (if the plant has given you permission to take them), and record spells and charms you've performed with the plant in question. You can refer to these templates year after year as your garden experience develops.

Section One

Getting Your
Garden
Started

A GREEN WITCH EMBRACES THE POWER of nature, draws energy from the earth and the universe, and relies on stones, plants, flowers, and herbs for healing. With the help of this journal, you will be able to catalog and track the various herbs, flowers, and plants you're growing in your magical space and record how you intend to use them in your witchcraft practice.

Every green thumb needs a place to write their garden secrets, even green witches! With this journal you finally have a place to record all of your garden progress and secrets, making a log of how you've cultivated your magical space. You'll be able to see what you've planted, when it's bloomed, how much water and light it needs, what its magical use is, and more. Your witchcraft practice has never been greener!

But first let's remember that a great garden starts with a great plan, and gardening as a green witch involves intention—which usually starts before the first seed goes into soil. Planning your garden can be as simple as laying rope or even a hose on the ground to mark out your beds, or you can draw out the garden on paper or even use garden design software. However you do it, deciding ahead of time what type of garden you want to grow and then carefully planning your magical space will give you the best chance of success.

Know Your Growing Environment

Your planning begins with learning about your environment, whether you're growing in containers inside or planning an ambitious outdoor garden. This kind of connection to the earth is central to the practice of green witchcraft, so taking this time to better understand your growing conditions will ultimately increase your magical skills.

Temperature

There are numerous tools and resources that can help you understand what types of plants will be successful in your area, beginning with the growing zones established by different countries, which will help you learn about your region's temperatures. USDA zones are classified according to the average low temperatures in the winters—the higher the zone, the warmer the winter temperatures. Zone 1, the very coldest, has an average annual winter minimum temperature of -60°F to -55°F. At the other end, zone 13 has an average winter minimum temperature of 60°F to 70°F.

Rainfall

Although temperature is certainly one of the most important factors, there are others you should consider, including how much annual rainfall your region gets and what kind of soil you have. Even in places that have roughly the same temperatures, how much rain falls will make a huge difference in which plants will grow best there. For example, Los Angeles gets about 15" of rainfall per year, while another warm city, Miami, gets about 62" of rain a year. Plants that thrive in rainy Miami would struggle in more arid Los Angeles. Average rainfall is especially important in an era of drought and climate change—many arid regions are restricting how much water is available for irrigation, including watering gardens and lawns.

Soil Type

Soil types generally range from sandy—especially in arid regions in the western and southwestern United States—to the loamy black soil of the Midwest or the rocky clay of New England. Again, the soil type matters because trying to grow a plant that evolved in the desert in heavy clay soil that holds water will be much harder than simply choosing a plant that thrives in those conditions.

If you're not certain about what type of soil you have, your local county extension office is a great resource. The vast majority of counties in the United States have an agricultural extension office that serves the county. These extension offices often have volunteers to answer questions or publish materials that are designed to help you understand your regional climate.

Microclimates

The final consideration in your planning is learning about your very specific planting conditions. This is often referred to as a microclimate, and it means just like it sounds: the climate in the exact area where you are planning a garden. Believe it or not, your microclimate might vary from your front yard to your backyard. You should consider other plants in the region, the local elevation (low or depressed areas will tend to be soggier than hilltops), and especially how much sun your planting area gets (a heavily shaded yard is a very different growing climate than an open pasture).

As you're evaluating your growing area, try to pay attention through as many seasons as possible. How does the level of sunlight change as spring eases into summer? If you live in a colder climate, when does the ground thaw? When is the first frost?

All of this can seem like a lot of planning when all you want to do is get your hands in the soil, but planning ahead of time will pay off in the long run. One of the truest axioms in gardening is a simple saying:

"Right plant, right place." By understanding your place, you'll be far ahead in choosing the right plants.

The good news is that you'll only have to do all this research once. After you've got your first garden planted, you can use this journal to keep records throughout the growing season. Over time, your garden journal will be your best resource, because you'll easily be able to flip through previous growing seasons and see what worked and what didn't.

Making Your Plan

Once you have your information ready, you can start planning your garden space. The shape and style of your garden should support your magical practice and channel energy. You can learn more about garden shapes and styles in *The Green Witch's Garden*.

Some of the meaningful garden designs green witches turn to include:

- **Astrological Gardens:** This design is based on the seven classical planets and often separates the planting space into zones that are associated with each of them. This garden shape can be circular, with zones marked out like slices of pizza, or rectangular and split into even zones.
- **Moon Gardens:** A moon garden focuses on the phases of the moon, both in shape and through your choice of plants. Designed to be viewed at night and day alike, the moon garden can be a circle or rectangular patch, with zones dedicated to different phases of the moon and different types of plants.

❧ **Elemental Gardens:** The elemental garden pays homage to the four elements of earth, water, fire, and air. These elements are equally important to the practice of witchcraft and to gardening. Once again, the shape of the garden can be circular, or a bordered patch shaped like a rectangle or square.

Beyond these spaces, there is no limit to what you can do with your garden design. Magic is inherent in every natural space and shape—you are only bound by your imagination and the natural rules of your environment. Depending on what type of energy you want to create, you can plan free-flowing wildflower beds, raised beds for vegetables, a more formal grid, or whatever shape speaks to you.

As you're planning, look to your space for inspiration. Large rocks or old stumps can be incorporated into your design. Natural features like sloping hillsides and streams can provide a spark for your imagination.

Once you know what type of magical garden you want to create, it's time to take some measurements of your space and draw the beds. You can use the blank grid pages in the back of this book to sketch out your garden, along with its zones and their meaning.

This is also a good time to think about features you'd like to include in the garden. Green witches often include protective measures, amulets, and other objects in their gardens to enhance their magic. This might mean placing mirrors to redirect bad fortune, protective statues, hanging glass balls, images of the Green Man, fairy lights, and water features. Each of these can have a role in the green witch's garden, so thinking about them in advance and being intentional in how you plan your design will ensure your garden is the sacred space you hope for.

Adding Practical Features

The final element of preparation includes planning for any practical features you want in your garden. This includes garden paths, lighting, and any accessibility features. At this stage, you don't need to make every decision about your features—if you don't know if you want a path made from gravel or slate stones, that's fine. The important part is to know where things are going. For lighting, you can plan to use solar lights that draw power from the sun, traditional landscape lights, or even torches or fire elements. If you're using traditional

A Magical Container Garden

If you don't have land or room for an ambitious outdoor garden, no worries: You can create a magical indoor garden in a terrarium or grow plants with magical properties in containers, especially herbs (many of which have extensive magical properties). Even houseplants like philodendron and spider plants can be incorporated into your magical practice.

Container gardens have the advantage of allowing you to control the location, soil quality, and watering to a much greater degree than your outdoor garden patch. They can be located indoors or used as focal points in your outdoor garden.

Though they have many advantages, container gardens do present some unique challenges because everything the plant needs must be provided, including water. In fact, watering mistakes are likely the number one killer of container plants, either by underwatering and starving the plants or overwatering and drowning them.

landscape lights, you'll need to run low-voltage wires underground and get access to electricity to plug in the transformer. An electrician or landscape contractor can help plan this type of element.

Once the layout is designed, it's time to prepare the beds. Depending on what you're doing, this may involve building structures like pergolas or supports for climbing plants, creating paths and borders, building raised beds, and placing features like lights and fountains. This is the time to run electrical and sprinkler lines if you need them.

This is also the time to start with any soil improvement you need. Ideally, you will be choosing plants that thrive in your local environment, but even in the healthiest soil, a little preparation can make a big difference. This might mean turning the soil over to loosen and aerate it, or it might mean mixing additions like compost or peat into the soil to improve the nutrient profile in your garden bed.

Finally, if your plan allows it, consider adding a thick layer of mulch to the beds. Lowly mulch might just be the gardener's best friend. It helps soil retain moisture, discourages weeds and pests, and helps hold the soil in place through the season. If you haven't already seen the benefits of a thick mulching, prepare to be pleasantly surprised.

Choosing Your Plants

With your plan in place, it's finally time to select plants. The selection of plants is one of the most critical elements in your green witch's garden. Not only do you want plants that will thrive in your region and microclimate, but your plants should also aid you in the types of spells and magic you want to perform.

When choosing plants, always look for ones that are proven to thrive in your area without extraordinary effort. It's tempting for witches to want lush, fairy-tale gardens bursting with color and texture, but that may not be possible in your area without intensive improvement to the soil and excessive use of water and fertilizer. Even if it's technically possible, this type of gardening is the opposite of how we approach the earth as green witches. We want to work with the land, not against it. We aim for balance and harmony, rather than subjugating nature under a blanket of chemicals and gadgets.

Instead, look for native plants that thrive with less intervention in your area, using the environmental profile you put together in the planning stage. Additionally, you can find lists of magical plants in *The Green Witch's Garden*, with information on how to grow each.

When it comes time to pick plants, here are a few tips:

- **Go to reputable local nurseries whenever possible.** It's true you can buy many plants from big-box stores, but a local nursery will have the expertise to give good advice and will often carry plants that are hard to find, unlike a chain store that orders nationally.
- **Don't be afraid to pop a plant out of its container to look at the roots.** Avoid transplants that are root-bound, or cuttings that have been transplanted so recently they don't have a good root structure. Look for plants with a healthy ball of white, firm roots.
- **Check new plants for pests and diseases before you bring them home.** Nurseries can have pest problems just like you can, and you don't want to bring a problem into your garden.

ॐ **Try to buy your plants as close to your planting date as possible.** If you're planning a new garden with a lot of transplants, you don't want to lose plants while you're waiting to complete the beds. Have the garden bed prepared, then buy plants and get them into the ground within twenty-four to forty-eight hours, if possible.

Whether you're using nursery plants or seedlings you grew yourself, when it comes time to plant, prepare your tools and give yourself enough time to plant the garden. It can be helpful in a new garden to set the pots out on the ground where the plant will eventually go into the dirt. There are no hard-and-fast rules that cover every plant, but make sure to space your plants far enough apart that they won't be crowded when they're adults. A common mistake gardeners make is to want a big "instant garden" and plant everything too close together. This increases the risk of pests and diseases later on, and your plants won't be as healthy.

During the actual planting, try not to bury plants too deep—this can be deadly for tender transplants. And be gentle with the roots and young stems. If the root balls are tight and you see a mass of knotted white roots, gently loosen the root ball with your fingers and try not to destroy or remove any more roots than you need to.

After you've planted everything, it's usually a good idea to water the whole garden right away. The new roots will be thirsty, and your plants will appreciate a good drink (this is true even of succulents). Depending on your garden location and the plants you're growing, be prepared to continue daily or near-daily watering for the first few days or weeks. This period of transition from the nursery pot or transplant container to the ground is when your plants are most fragile—a little babying through this early period will go a long way toward having a successful season.

You should also water if you're direct-sowing seeds into the ground. Make sure to follow any label instructions for direct-sown seeds, but in most cases, they will appreciate the moisture to help them germinate and sprout.

Maintaining Your Garden

After your seeds or transplants are safely in the ground, you can sit back and take a well-earned rest. If you've taken the proper steps in planning, you've already set yourself up for success with your green witch's garden.

But don't plan on resting too long! A healthy garden isn't an accident—it's the product of preparation and good habits. Just like your pets or any living thing, your plants will thrive with proper attention paid to them. Once it's planted, try to visit your garden daily or most days. While you're there, you may:

> **Water your plants.** You may need to water daily, especially in the beginning. As the season wears on and the rains come, you might not need to water as much. You can tell water-stressed plants if they are drooping or limp. Record when you water and how much it rains in this journal for the future—you may be surprised how helpful it is to look back on previous seasons.

ॐ **Inspect for pests and diseases.** Simply paying attention to your plants is one of the best things you can do for your garden. Every time you're in the garden, try to really look at your plants closely. Flip leaves over to see if there are pests attacking your plants. Look for the telltale signs of problems, like fine webs spun around the base of leaves, black droppings from caterpillars or other munching insects, or chewing marks from beetles or slugs. Catching an issue early can make all the difference between success and failure, and it certainly makes it easier to handle the problem without resorting to chemicals.

Weekly Tasks

As time wears on, you'll have weekly tasks as well. Probably the most important task on your weekly list is weeding. Depending on where you're gardening and what types of weeds are in your area, the weeds can grow shockingly fast. But also remember that, as a green witch, not all surprise arrivals to your garden are weeds. Sometimes a plant may germinate from a wild seed that has powerful magical properties. After all, what's a weed except a plant growing where you don't want it to grow? If you do see unwanted weeds start popping up in your bed, pluck them out of the soil and dispose of them, roots and all. Once again, staying on top of the weeding early will make it much less likely that you'll be out in your garden in the fall with a hoe or pitchfork battling an invasion of waist-high weeds.

Depending on what you're growing, you can also use your weekly maintenance visits to tie up vines and train your vegetables. Some plants, like tomatoes and beans, prefer to grow on frames or structures. Securely tie up the new growth and snip away any suckers (pesky branches that grow upright or emerge from between the leaf stalk and stem and tend to draw away energy from the plant so it will yield less or grow less vigorously).

Monthly Tasks

Finally, there are the tasks you'll do monthly or maybe just a few times all season, including pruning larger branches on woody shrubs or trees and training your plants. Again, depending on what you're growing, you might need to plan for some time in your garden with a pair of loppers (pruning shears) or a saw to cut away woody suckers or prune away excessive growth. This can be hard work, so keep a good pair of gloves handy.

Fertilizing your garden is also likely to be a monthly task. If you've prepared your beds with healthy, aerated soil and picked plants that thrive in your area, hopefully you won't need to apply too much fertilizer—but there's no question that fertilizer can be the difference between a good garden and an amazing one. That said, you may not need to spend a fortune on a specialized liquid fertilizer. In many cases, a simple balanced, organic fertilizer with all of the necessary macronutrients is all you'll need. As always, before applying fertilizer or any type of chemical, carefully read the label and follow all safety instructions.

You might have noticed that I didn't include spraying or treating your garden in the list of regular tasks. It's true that many successful gardeners, and most farmers, rely on a cornucopia of chemicals to achieve their near-perfect results, but this is not in the spirit of the green witch garden. If you're planning on consuming any parts of your plants—such as herbs or vegetables—or burning them in spells and charms, you don't want to worry about introducing toxins into your magic.

Instead of regular spraying, I believe in taking the most natural approach and seeking balance. A well-planned garden will feature a mix of plants instead of a single species en masse that will attract pests. Additionally, if you're paying attention to your garden, you'll hopefully catch any problems early enough to take care of them in the lowest-impact way possible. It's amazing what a simple jet of water can do when it comes to knocking off pests before they can spread and destroy your garden.

Beyond that, if you have to use a chemical to treat your plants, always start with the least toxic option. Putting isopropyl rubbing alcohol on cotton swabs can control scale insects, for example, or consider horticultural oil or neem oil for bigger infestations. Whatever you do, always read the product labels carefully and take any recommended safety precautions.

As always, keep good notes in your journal as the season goes on. Your journal will become an invaluable resource as seasons go by, creating a permanent record of the unique conditions in your microclimate and how you were best able to control the pests in your area.

Harvest Time

One of the great joys of gardening is getting to harvest the fruits of your labor. When you harvest will be determined by the types of plants you're growing. In your green witch's garden, you might be growing herbs that can be clipped for leaves almost as soon as they're established, or maybe you're growing vegetables that have a longer ripening time before they're ready to be picked and used. Your best guide to harvesting will be instructions specific to the plants themselves. That being said, there are a few universal things you want to keep in mind when approaching harvesting.

First, if these are plants you plan on consuming and you're using any kind of chemical controls, make sure to stop using the chemicals on your plants in the recommended time frame. You can find this information on the chemical label under "safety precautions." For many pesticides, you will be instructed to stop using the chemical within a few days to a week or more before harvest. The same might apply to fertilizers, again depending on what you're growing and what fertilizers you're using.

When you do harvest, use clean tools and don't damage the fruit or leaves in the process. Sharp garden shears are an essential tool throughout the season, but they're invaluable when it's time to snip ripe tomatoes off the vine or clip fresh herbs. It's almost always better to snip your harvest away rather than twist or tug on leaves or fruit. For root vegetables, use a good trowel to first loosen the soil, then gently remove the root from the dirt.

It's also recommended to harvest most plants when they are dry. This will help prevent fungus and rot in the newly harvested vegetables. Once harvested, it's perfectly okay to wash your vegetables, always taking care not to bruise them and drying them completely afterward. If you have an old laundry basket with holes, you can place the newly harvested vegetables in there for a quick rinse as you're working. Use the coldest water you have to prevent the vegetables from warming up before you have a chance to get them inside.

After you're done with the harvest, your work for the season can start winding down as you prepare for colder weather. Remove any annuals; trim away the last of the suckers on your trees and prepare them for the long rest of fall and winter; and clean away any random debris. This is a good time to thank your garden for the bounty it's brought throughout the season and to make any final notes in your journal about the season.

And, of course, it's never too early to start planning for next year!

Section Two

A Weekly Journal

Weekly Log

ASTROLOGICAL NOTES
(E.g., Sun sign, Moon sign, astrological events.)

_____

_____

_____

_____

_____

_____

_____

	TEMPS *High/Low*	RAINFALL *Inches*
M	/	
T	/	
W	/	
T	/	
F	/	
S	/	
S	/	

TO-DO ITEMS

- Fertilize
- Harvest
- Weed
- Prune
- _____
- _____
- _____
- _____
- _____
- _____
- _____

OBSERVED

- Wildlife
- Bees/Other Pollinators
- Butterflies
- Dragonflies
- Ladybugs
- Birds/Hummingbirds
- Diseased or Sick Plants
- _____
- _____
- _____
- _____
- _____

DAILY NOTES
Record your activity here, along with notes on how your plants are growing or about the weather. Record the moon phases in the circles.

M

T

W

T

F

S

S

Weekly Log

ASTROLOGICAL NOTES
(E.g., Sun sign, Moon sign, astrological events.)

	TEMPS *High/Low*	RAINFALL *Inches*
M	/	
T	/	
W	/	
T	/	
F	/	
S	/	
S	/	

_____

_____

_____

_____

_____

_____

_____

TO-DO ITEMS

- Fertilize
- Harvest
- Weed
- Prune
- _____
- _____
- _____
- _____
- _____
- _____
- _____

OBSERVED

- Wildlife
- Bees/Other Pollinators
- Butterflies
- Dragonflies
- Ladybugs
- Birds/Hummingbirds
- Diseased or Sick Plants
- _____
- _____
- _____
- _____

DAILY NOTES

Record your activity here, along with notes on how your plants are growing or about the weather. Record the moon phases in the circles.

M ○

T ○

W ○

T ○

F ○

S ○

S ○

Weekly Log

ASTROLOGICAL NOTES
(E.g., Sun sign, Moon sign, astrological events.)

	TEMPS	RAINFALL
	High/Low	*Inches*
M	/	
T	/	
W	/	
T	/	
F	/	
S	/	
S	/	

TO-DO ITEMS

- Fertilize
- Harvest
- Weed
- Prune
- _____
- _____
- _____
- _____
- _____
- _____
- _____

OBSERVED

- Wildlife
- Bees/Other Pollinators
- Butterflies
- Dragonflies
- Ladybugs
- Birds/Hummingbirds
- Diseased or Sick Plants
- _____
- _____
- _____
- _____
- _____

DAILY NOTES
Record your activity here, along with notes on how your plants are growing or about the weather. Record the moon phases in the circles.

M
○

T
○

W
○

T
○

F
○

S
○

S
○

Weekly Log

ASTROLOGICAL NOTES
(E.g., Sun sign, Moon sign, astrological events.)

_____

_____

_____

_____

_____

_____

_____

	TEMPS _High/Low_	RAINFALL _Inches_
M	/	
T	/	
W	/	
T	/	
F	/	
S	/	
S	/	

TO-DO ITEMS

- Fertilize
- Harvest
- Weed
- Prune
- _____
- _____
- _____
- _____
- _____
- _____

OBSERVED

- Wildlife
- Bees/Other Pollinators
- Butterflies
- Dragonflies
- Ladybugs
- Birds/Hummingbirds
- Diseased or Sick Plants
- _____
- _____
- _____
- _____

DAILY NOTES

Record your activity here, along with notes on how your plants are growing or about the weather. Record the moon phases in the circles.

M

T

W

T

F

S

S

Weekly Log

ASTROLOGICAL NOTES
(E.g., Sun sign, Moon sign, astrological events.)

	TEMPS	RAINFALL
	High/Low	*Inches*

_____

_____

_____

_____

_____

_____

_____

	TEMPS High/Low	RAINFALL Inches
M	/	
T	/	
W	/	
T	/	
F	/	
S	/	
S	/	

TO-DO ITEMS

Fertilize

Harvest

Weed

Prune

_____

_____

_____

_____

_____

_____

_____

OBSERVED

Wildlife

Bees/Other Pollinators

Butterflies

Dragonflies

Ladybugs

Birds/Hummingbirds

Diseased or Sick Plants

_____

_____

_____

_____

DAILY NOTES

Record your activity here, along with notes on how your plants are growing or about the weather. Record the moon phases in the circles.

M ○

T ○

W ○

T ○

F ○

S ○

S ○

Weekly Log

ASTROLOGICAL NOTES
(E.g., Sun sign, Moon sign, astrological events.)

_____

_____

_____

_____

_____

_____

_____

	TEMPS _High/Low_	RAINFALL _Inches_
M	/	
T	/	
W	/	
T	/	
F	/	
S	/	
S	/	

TO-DO ITEMS

- Fertilize
- Harvest
- Weed
- Prune
- _____
- _____
- _____
- _____
- _____
- _____
- _____
- _____

OBSERVED

- Wildlife
- Bees/Other Pollinators
- Butterflies
- Dragonflies
- Ladybugs
- Birds/Hummingbirds
- Diseased or Sick Plants
- _____
- _____
- _____
- _____
- _____

DAILY NOTES

Record your activity here, along with notes on how your plants are growing or about the weather. Record the moon phases in the circles.

M

T

W

T

F

S

S

Weekly Log

ASTROLOGICAL NOTES
(E.g., Sun sign, Moon sign, astrological events.)

	TEMPS *High/Low*	RAINFALL *Inches*
M	/	
T	/	
W	/	
T	/	
F	/	
S	/	
S	/	

_____

_____

_____

_____

_____

_____

_____

TO-DO ITEMS

- Fertilize
- Harvest
- Weed
- Prune
- _____
- _____
- _____
- _____
- _____
- _____
- _____
- _____

OBSERVED

- Wildlife
- Bees/Other Pollinators
- Butterflies
- Dragonflies
- Ladybugs
- Birds/Hummingbirds
- Diseased or Sick Plants
- _____
- _____
- _____
- _____
- _____

DAILY NOTES

Record your activity here, along with notes on how your plants are growing or about the weather. Record the moon phases in the circles.

M ○

T ○

W ○

T ○

F ○

S ○

S ○

Weekly Log

ASTROLOGICAL NOTES
(E.g., Sun sign, Moon sign, astrological events.)

	TEMPS *High/Low*	RAINFALL *Inches*
M	/	
T	/	
W	/	
T	/	
F	/	
S	/	
S	/	

_____

_____

_____

_____

_____

_____

_____

TO-DO ITEMS

- Fertilize
- Harvest
- Weed
- Prune
- _____
- _____
- _____
- _____
- _____
- _____
- _____
- _____

OBSERVED

- Wildlife
- Bees/Other Pollinators
- Butterflies
- Dragonflies
- Ladybugs
- Birds/Hummingbirds
- Diseased or Sick Plants
- _____
- _____
- _____
- _____
- _____

DAILY NOTES

Record your activity here, along with notes on how your plants are growing or about the weather. Record the moon phases in the circles.

M

T

W

T

F

S

S

Weekly Log

ASTROLOGICAL NOTES
(E.g., Sun sign, Moon sign, astrological events.)

_____

_____

_____

_____

_____

_____

_____

	TEMPS	RAINFALL
	High/Low	*Inches*
M	/	
T	/	
W	/	
T	/	
F	/	
S	/	
S	/	

TO-DO ITEMS

- Fertilize
- Harvest
- Weed
- Prune
- _____
- _____
- _____
- _____
- _____
- _____
- _____

OBSERVED

- Wildlife
- Bees/Other Pollinators
- Butterflies
- Dragonflies
- Ladybugs
- Birds/Hummingbirds
- Diseased or Sick Plants
- _____
- _____
- _____

DAILY NOTES

Record your activity here, along with notes on how your plants are growing or about the weather. Record the moon phases in the circles.

M

T

W

T

F

S

S

Weekly Log

ASTROLOGICAL NOTES
(E.g., Sun sign, Moon sign, astrological events.)

	TEMPS High/Low	RAINFALL Inches
M	/	
T	/	
W	/	
T	/	
F	/	
S	/	
S	/	

_____

_____

_____

_____

_____

_____

_____

TO-DO ITEMS

- Fertilize
- Harvest
- Weed
- Prune
- _____
- _____
- _____
- _____
- _____
- _____
- _____
- _____

OBSERVED

- Wildlife
- Bees/Other Pollinators
- Butterflies
- Dragonflies
- Ladybugs
- Birds/Hummingbirds
- Diseased or Sick Plants
- _____
- _____
- _____
- _____
- _____

DAILY NOTES

Record your activity here, along with notes on how your plants are growing or about the weather. Record the moon phases in the circles.

M ○

T ○

W ○

T ○

F ○

S ○

S ○

Weekly Log

ASTROLOGICAL NOTES
(E.g., Sun sign, Moon sign, astrological events.)

_____

_____

_____

_____

_____

_____

_____

	TEMPS High/Low	RAINFALL Inches
M	/	
T	/	
W	/	
T	/	
F	/	
S	/	
S	/	

TO-DO ITEMS

- Fertilize
- Harvest
- Weed
- Prune
- _____
- _____
- _____
- _____
- _____
- _____
- _____

OBSERVED

- Wildlife
- Bees/Other Pollinators
- Butterflies
- Dragonflies
- Ladybugs
- Birds/Hummingbirds
- Diseased or Sick Plants
- _____
- _____
- _____
- _____

DAILY NOTES
Record your activity here, along with notes on how your plants are
growing or about the weather. Record the moon phases in the circles.

M

T

W

T

F

S

S

Weekly Log

ASTROLOGICAL NOTES
(E.g., Sun sign, Moon sign, astrological events.)

_____

_____

_____

_____

_____

_____

_____

	TEMPS High/Low	RAINFALL Inches
M	/	
T	/	
W	/	
T	/	
F	/	
S	/	
S	/	

TO-DO ITEMS

- Fertilize
- Harvest
- Weed
- Prune
- _____
- _____
- _____
- _____
- _____
- _____
- _____
- _____

OBSERVED

- Wildlife
- Bees/Other Pollinators
- Butterflies
- Dragonflies
- Ladybugs
- Birds/Hummingbirds
- Diseased or Sick Plants
- _____
- _____
- _____
- _____
- _____

DAILY NOTES

Record your activity here, along with notes on how your plants are growing or about the weather. Record the moon phases in the circles.

M ○

T ○

W ○

T ○

F ○

S ○

S ○

Weekly Log

ASTROLOGICAL NOTES
(E.g., Sun sign, Moon sign, astrological events.)

	TEMPS	RAINFALL
	High/Low	*Inches*
M	/	
T	/	
W	/	
T	/	
F	/	
S	/	
S	/	

_____

_____

_____

_____

_____

_____

_____

TO-DO ITEMS

- Fertilize
- Harvest
- Weed
- Prune
- _____
- _____
- _____
- _____
- _____
- _____
- _____
- _____

OBSERVED

- Wildlife
- Bees/Other Pollinators
- Butterflies
- Dragonflies
- Ladybugs
- Birds/Hummingbirds
- Diseased or Sick Plants
- _____
- _____
- _____
- _____
- _____

DAILY NOTES

Record your activity here, along with notes on how your plants are growing or about the weather. Record the moon phases in the circles.

M

T

W

T

F

S

S

FROM / / **TO** / /

Weekly Log

ASTROLOGICAL NOTES
(E.g., Sun sign, Moon sign, astrological events.)

_____

_____

_____

_____

_____

_____

_____

	TEMPS _High/Low_	RAINFALL _Inches_
M	/	
T	/	
W	/	
T	/	
F	/	
S	/	
S	/	

TO-DO ITEMS

- Fertilize
- Harvest
- Weed
- Prune
- _____
- _____
- _____
- _____
- _____
- _____
- _____

OBSERVED

- Wildlife
- Bees/Other Pollinators
- Butterflies
- Dragonflies
- Ladybugs
- Birds/Hummingbirds
- Diseased or Sick Plants
- _____
- _____
- _____
- _____
- _____

DAILY NOTES

Record your activity here, along with notes on how your plants are growing or about the weather. Record the moon phases in the circles.

M ◯

T ◯

W ◯

T ◯

F ◯

S ◯

S ◯

Weekly Log

ASTROLOGICAL NOTES
(E.g., Sun sign, Moon sign, astrological events.)

_____

_____

_____

_____

_____

_____

_____

	TEMPS _High/Low_	RAINFALL _Inches_
M	/	
T	/	
W	/	
T	/	
F	/	
S	/	
S	/	

TO-DO ITEMS

- Fertilize
- Harvest
- Weed
- Prune
- _____
- _____
- _____
- _____
- _____
- _____
- _____
- _____

OBSERVED

- Wildlife
- Bees/Other Pollinators
- Butterflies
- Dragonflies
- Ladybugs
- Birds/Hummingbirds
- Diseased or Sick Plants
- _____
- _____
- _____
- _____
- _____

DAILY NOTES

Record your activity here, along with notes on how your plants are growing or about the weather. Record the moon phases in the circles.

M ○

T ○

W ○

T ○

F ○

S ○

S ○

Weekly Log

ASTROLOGICAL NOTES
(E.g., Sun sign, Moon sign, astrological events.)

	TEMPS	RAINFALL
	High/Low	*Inches*
M	/	
T	/	
W	/	
T	/	
F	/	
S	/	
S	/	

TO-DO ITEMS

- Fertilize
- Harvest
- Weed
- Prune
- _____
- _____
- _____
- _____
- _____
- _____
- _____
- _____

OBSERVED

- Wildlife
- Bees/Other Pollinators
- Butterflies
- Dragonflies
- Ladybugs
- Birds/Hummingbirds
- Diseased or Sick Plants
- _____
- _____
- _____
- _____

DAILY NOTES

Record your activity here, along with notes on how your plants are growing or about the weather. Record the moon phases in the circles.

M

T

W

T

F

S

S

Weekly Log

ASTROLOGICAL NOTES
(E.g., Sun sign, Moon sign, astrological events.)

_____
_____
_____
_____
_____
_____
_____

	TEMPS High/Low	RAINFALL Inches
M	/	
T	/	
W	/	
T	/	
F	/	
S	/	
S	/	

TO-DO ITEMS

- Fertilize
- Harvest
- Weed
- Prune
- _____
- _____
- _____
- _____
- _____
- _____
- _____

OBSERVED

- Wildlife
- Bees/Other Pollinators
- Butterflies
- Dragonflies
- Ladybugs
- Birds/Hummingbirds
- Diseased or Sick Plants
- _____
- _____
- _____
- _____

DAILY NOTES

Record your activity here, along with notes on how your plants are growing or about the weather. Record the moon phases in the circles.

M

T

W

T

F

S

S

Weekly Log

ASTROLOGICAL NOTES
(E.g., Sun sign, Moon sign, astrological events.)

	TEMPS _High/Low_	RAINFALL _Inches_
M	/	
T	/	
W	/	
T	/	
F	/	
S	/	
S	/	

TO-DO ITEMS

- Fertilize
- Harvest
- Weed
- Prune
-
-
-
-
-
-
-

OBSERVED

- Wildlife
- Bees/Other Pollinators
- Butterflies
- Dragonflies
- Ladybugs
- Birds/Hummingbirds
- Diseased or Sick Plants
-
-
-
-

DAILY NOTES

Record your activity here, along with notes on how your plants are growing or about the weather. Record the moon phases in the circles.

M

T

W

T

F

S

S

Weekly Log

ASTROLOGICAL NOTES
(E.g., Sun sign, Moon sign, astrological events.)

_____

_____

_____

_____

_____

_____

_____

	TEMPS High/Low	RAINFALL Inches
M	/	
T	/	
W	/	
T	/	
F	/	
S	/	
S	/	

TO-DO ITEMS

- Fertilize
- Harvest
- Weed
- Prune
- _____
- _____
- _____
- _____
- _____
- _____
- _____

OBSERVED

- Wildlife
- Bees/Other Pollinators
- Butterflies
- Dragonflies
- Ladybugs
- Birds/Hummingbirds
- Diseased or Sick Plants
- _____
- _____
- _____
- _____

DAILY NOTES
Record your activity here, along with notes on how your plants are
growing or about the weather. Record the moon phases in the circles.

M

T

W

T

F

S

S

Weekly Log

ASTROLOGICAL NOTES
(E.g., Sun sign, Moon sign, astrological events.)

_____

_____

_____

_____

_____

_____

_____

	TEMPS High/Low	RAINFALL Inches
M	/	
T	/	
W	/	
T	/	
F	/	
S	/	
S	/	

TO-DO ITEMS

- Fertilize
- Harvest
- Weed
- Prune
- _____
- _____
- _____
- _____
- _____
- _____
- _____
- _____

OBSERVED

- Wildlife
- Bees/Other Pollinators
- Butterflies
- Dragonflies
- Ladybugs
- Birds/Hummingbirds
- Diseased or Sick Plants
- _____
- _____
- _____
- _____

DAILY NOTES

Record your activity here, along with notes on how your plants are growing or about the weather. Record the moon phases in the circles.

M

T

W

T

F

S

S

Weekly Log

ASTROLOGICAL NOTES
(E.g., Sun sign, Moon sign, astrological events.)

_____

_____

_____

_____

_____

_____

_____

	TEMPS High/Low	RAINFALL Inches
M	/	
T	/	
W	/	
T	/	
F	/	
S	/	
S	/	

TO-DO ITEMS

- Fertilize
- Harvest
- Weed
- Prune
- _____
- _____
- _____
- _____
- _____
- _____
- _____
- _____

OBSERVED

- Wildlife
- Bees/Other Pollinators
- Butterflies
- Dragonflies
- Ladybugs
- Birds/Hummingbirds
- Diseased or Sick Plants
- _____
- _____
- _____
- _____
- _____

DAILY NOTES

Record your activity here, along with notes on how your plants are growing or about the weather. Record the moon phases in the circles.

M
○

T
○

W
○

T
○

F
○

S
○

S
○

Weekly Log

ASTROLOGICAL NOTES
(E.g., Sun sign, Moon sign, astrological events.)

_____

_____

_____

_____

_____

_____

_____

	TEMPS High/Low	RAINFALL Inches
M	/	
T	/	
W	/	
T	/	
F	/	
S	/	
S	/	

TO-DO ITEMS

- Fertilize
- Harvest
- Weed
- Prune
- _____
- _____
- _____
- _____
- _____
- _____
- _____
- _____

OBSERVED

- Wildlife
- Bees/Other Pollinators
- Butterflies
- Dragonflies
- Ladybugs
- Birds/Hummingbirds
- Diseased or Sick Plants
- _____
- _____
- _____
- _____
- _____

DAILY NOTES

Record your activity here, along with notes on how your plants are growing or about the weather. Record the moon phases in the circles.

M ○

T ○

W ○

T ○

F ○

S ○

S ○

Weekly Log

ASTROLOGICAL NOTES
(E.g., Sun sign, Moon sign, astrological events.)

_____

_____

_____

_____

_____

_____

_____

	TEMPS High/Low	RAINFALL Inches
M	/	
T	/	
W	/	
T	/	
F	/	
S	/	
S	/	

TO-DO ITEMS

- Fertilize
- Harvest
- Weed
- Prune
- _____
- _____
- _____
- _____
- _____
- _____
- _____
- _____

OBSERVED

- Wildlife
- Bees/Other Pollinators
- Butterflies
- Dragonflies
- Ladybugs
- Birds/Hummingbirds
- Diseased or Sick Plants
- _____
- _____
- _____
- _____
- _____

DAILY NOTES

Record your activity here, along with notes on how your plants are growing or about the weather. Record the moon phases in the circles.

M

T

W

T

F

S

S

Weekly Log

ASTROLOGICAL NOTES
(E.g., Sun sign, Moon sign, astrological events.)

_____

_____

_____

_____

_____

_____

_____

	TEMPS _High/Low_	RAINFALL _Inches_
M	/	
T	/	
W	/	
T	/	
F	/	
S	/	
S	/	

TO-DO ITEMS

- Fertilize
- Harvest
- Weed
- Prune
- _____
- _____
- _____
- _____
- _____
- _____
- _____
- _____

OBSERVED

- Wildlife
- Bees/Other Pollinators
- Butterflies
- Dragonflies
- Ladybugs
- Birds/Hummingbirds
- Diseased or Sick Plants
- _____
- _____
- _____
- _____
- _____

DAILY NOTES

Record your activity here, along with notes on how your plants are growing or about the weather. Record the moon phases in the circles.

M

T

W

T

F

S

S

Weekly Log

ASTROLOGICAL NOTES
(E.g., Sun sign, Moon sign, astrological events.)

_____

_____

_____

_____

_____

_____

_____

	TEMPS High/Low	RAINFALL Inches
M	/	
T	/	
W	/	
T	/	
F	/	
S	/	
S	/	

TO-DO ITEMS

- Fertilize
- Harvest
- Weed
- Prune
- _____
- _____
- _____
- _____
- _____
- _____
- _____
- _____

OBSERVED

- Wildlife
- Bees/Other Pollinators
- Butterflies
- Dragonflies
- Ladybugs
- Birds/Hummingbirds
- Diseased or Sick Plants
- _____
- _____
- _____
- _____

DAILY NOTES

Record your activity here, along with notes on how your plants are growing or about the weather. Record the moon phases in the circles.

M ○ _____

T ○ _____

W ○ _____

T ○ _____

F ○ _____

S ○ _____

S ○ _____

Weekly Log

ASTROLOGICAL NOTES
(E.g., Sun sign, Moon sign, astrological events.)

_____

_____

_____

_____

_____

_____

_____

	TEMPS High/Low	RAINFALL Inches
M	/	
T	/	
W	/	
T	/	
F	/	
S	/	
S	/	

TO-DO ITEMS

- Fertilize
- Harvest
- Weed
- Prune
- _____
- _____
- _____
- _____
- _____
- _____
- _____

OBSERVED

- Wildlife
- Bees/Other Pollinators
- Butterflies
- Dragonflies
- Ladybugs
- Birds/Hummingbirds
- Diseased or Sick Plants
- _____
- _____
- _____
- _____

DAILY NOTES

Record your activity here, along with notes on how your plants are growing or about the weather. Record the moon phases in the circles.

M

T

W

T

F

S

S

Weekly Log

ASTROLOGICAL NOTES
(E.g., Sun sign, Moon sign, astrological events.)

_____

_____

_____

_____

_____

_____

_____

	TEMPS High/Low	RAINFALL Inches
M	/	
T	/	
W	/	
T	/	
F	/	
S	/	
S	/	

TO-DO ITEMS

- Fertilize
- Harvest
- Weed
- Prune
- _____
- _____
- _____
- _____
- _____
- _____
- _____

OBSERVED

- Wildlife
- Bees/Other Pollinators
- Butterflies
- Dragonflies
- Ladybugs
- Birds/Hummingbirds
- Diseased or Sick Plants
- _____
- _____
- _____
- _____
- _____

DAILY NOTES

Record your activity here, along with notes on how your plants are growing or about the weather. Record the moon phases in the circles.

M

T

W

T

F

S

S

Weekly Log

ASTROLOGICAL NOTES
(E.g., Sun sign, Moon sign, astrological events.)

_____

_____

_____

_____

_____

_____

_____

	TEMPS _High/Low_	RAINFALL _Inches_
M	/	
T	/	
W	/	
T	/	
F	/	
S	/	
S	/	

TO-DO ITEMS

- Fertilize
- Harvest
- Weed
- Prune
- _____
- _____
- _____
- _____
- _____
- _____
- _____
- _____

OBSERVED

- Wildlife
- Bees/Other Pollinators
- Butterflies
- Dragonflies
- Ladybugs
- Birds/Hummingbirds
- Diseased or Sick Plants
- _____
- _____
- _____
- _____
- _____

DAILY NOTES

Record your activity here, along with notes on how your plants are growing or about the weather. Record the moon phases in the circles.

M ○

T ○

W ○

T ○

F ○

S ○

S ○

Weekly Log

ASTROLOGICAL NOTES
(E.g., Sun sign, Moon sign, astrological events.)

_____

_____

_____

_____

_____

_____

_____

	TEMPS High/Low	RAINFALL Inches
M	/	
T	/	
W	/	
T	/	
F	/	
S	/	
S	/	

TO-DO ITEMS

- Fertilize
- Harvest
- Weed
- Prune
- _____
- _____
- _____
- _____
- _____
- _____
- _____
- _____

OBSERVED

- Wildlife
- Bees/Other Pollinators
- Butterflies
- Dragonflies
- Ladybugs
- Birds/Hummingbirds
- Diseased or Sick Plants
- _____
- _____
- _____
- _____
- _____

DAILY NOTES

Record your activity here, along with notes on how your plants are growing or about the weather. Record the moon phases in the circles.

M

T

W

T

F

S

S

Weekly Log

ASTROLOGICAL NOTES
(E.g., Sun sign, Moon sign, astrological events.)

_____

_____

_____

_____

_____

_____

_____

	TEMPS High/Low	RAINFALL Inches
M	/	
T	/	
W	/	
T	/	
F	/	
S	/	
S	/	

TO-DO ITEMS

- Fertilize
- Harvest
- Weed
- Prune
- _____
- _____
- _____
- _____
- _____
- _____
- _____

OBSERVED

- Wildlife
- Bees/Other Pollinators
- Butterflies
- Dragonflies
- Ladybugs
- Birds/Hummingbirds
- Diseased or Sick Plants
- _____
- _____
- _____
- _____
- _____

DAILY NOTES

Record your activity here, along with notes on how your plants are growing or about the weather. Record the moon phases in the circles.

M ○

T ○

W ○

T ○

F ○

S ○

S ○

Weekly Log

ASTROLOGICAL NOTES
(E.g., Sun sign, Moon sign, astrological events.)

_____

_____

_____

_____

_____

_____

_____

	TEMPS *High/Low*	RAINFALL *Inches*
M	/	
T	/	
W	/	
T	/	
F	/	
S	/	
S	/	

TO-DO ITEMS

- Fertilize
- Harvest
- Weed
- Prune
- _____
- _____
- _____
- _____
- _____
- _____
- _____

OBSERVED

- Wildlife
- Bees/Other Pollinators
- Butterflies
- Dragonflies
- Ladybugs
- Birds/Hummingbirds
- Diseased or Sick Plants
- _____
- _____
- _____
- _____

DAILY NOTES

Record your activity here, along with notes on how your plants are growing or about the weather. Record the moon phases in the circles.

M

T

W

T

F

S

S

Weekly Log

ASTROLOGICAL NOTES
(E.g., Sun sign, Moon sign, astrological events.)

	TEMPS	RAINFALL
	High/Low	Inches
M	/	
T	/	
W	/	
T	/	
F	/	
S	/	
S	/	

TO-DO ITEMS

- Fertilize
- Harvest
- Weed
- Prune
-
-
-
-
-
-
-

OBSERVED

- Wildlife
- Bees/Other Pollinators
- Butterflies
- Dragonflies
- Ladybugs
- Birds/Hummingbirds
- Diseased or Sick Plants
-
-
-
-

DAILY NOTES

Record your activity here, along with notes on how your plants are growing or about the weather. Record the moon phases in the circles.

M

T

W

T

F

S

S

Weekly Log

ASTROLOGICAL NOTES
(E.g., Sun sign, Moon sign, astrological events.)

	TEMPS High/Low	RAINFALL Inches
M	/	
T	/	
W	/	
T	/	
F	/	
S	/	
S	/	

_____

_____

_____

_____

_____

_____

_____

TO-DO ITEMS

- Fertilize
- Harvest
- Weed
- Prune
- _____
- _____
- _____
- _____
- _____
- _____
- _____

OBSERVED

- Wildlife
- Bees/Other Pollinators
- Butterflies
- Dragonflies
- Ladybugs
- Birds/Hummingbirds
- Diseased or Sick Plants
- _____
- _____
- _____
- _____

DAILY NOTES

Record your activity here, along with notes on how your plants are growing or about the weather. Record the moon phases in the circles.

M

T

W

T

F

S

S

Weekly Log

ASTROLOGICAL NOTES
(E.g., Sun sign, Moon sign, astrological events.)

_____

_____

_____

_____

_____

_____

_____

	TEMPS High/Low	RAINFALL Inches
M	/	
T	/	
W	/	
T	/	
F	/	
S	/	
S	/	

TO-DO ITEMS

- Fertilize
- Harvest
- Weed
- Prune
- _____
- _____
- _____
- _____
- _____
- _____
- _____

OBSERVED

- Wildlife
- Bees/Other Pollinators
- Butterflies
- Dragonflies
- Ladybugs
- Birds/Hummingbirds
- Diseased or Sick Plants
- _____
- _____
- _____
- _____

DAILY NOTES

Record your activity here, along with notes on how your plants are growing or about the weather. Record the moon phases in the circles.

M

T

W

T

F

S

S

Weekly Log

ASTROLOGICAL NOTES
(E.g., Sun sign, Moon sign, astrological events.)

_____

_____

_____

_____

_____

_____

_____

	TEMPS High/Low	RAINFALL Inches
M	/	
T	/	
W	/	
T	/	
F	/	
S	/	
S	/	

TO-DO ITEMS

- Fertilize
- Harvest
- Weed
- Prune
- _____
- _____
- _____
- _____
- _____
- _____
- _____
- _____

OBSERVED

- Wildlife
- Bees/Other Pollinators
- Butterflies
- Dragonflies
- Ladybugs
- Birds/Hummingbirds
- Diseased or Sick Plants
- _____
- _____
- _____
- _____

DAILY NOTES

Record your activity here, along with notes on how your plants are growing or about the weather. Record the moon phases in the circles.

M

T

W

T

F

S

S

Weekly Log

ASTROLOGICAL NOTES
(E.g., Sun sign, Moon sign, astrological events.)

_____

_____

_____

_____

_____

_____

_____

	TEMPS High/Low	RAINFALL Inches
M	/	
T	/	
W	/	
T	/	
F	/	
S	/	
S	/	

TO-DO ITEMS

- Fertilize
- Harvest
- Weed
- Prune
- _____
- _____
- _____
- _____
- _____
- _____
- _____

OBSERVED

- Wildlife
- Bees/Other Pollinators
- Butterflies
- Dragonflies
- Ladybugs
- Birds/Hummingbirds
- Diseased or Sick Plants
- _____
- _____
- _____
- _____
- _____

DAILY NOTES

Record your activity here, along with notes on how your plants are growing or about the weather. Record the moon phases in the circles.

M

T

W

T

F

S

S

Weekly Log

ASTROLOGICAL NOTES
(E.g., Sun sign, Moon sign, astrological events.)

	TEMPS High/Low	RAINFALL Inches
M	/	
T	/	
W	/	
T	/	
F	/	
S	/	
S	/	

_____

_____

_____

_____

_____

_____

_____

TO-DO ITEMS

- Fertilize
- Harvest
- Weed
- Prune
- _____
- _____
- _____
- _____
- _____
- _____
- _____

OBSERVED

- Wildlife
- Bees/Other Pollinators
- Butterflies
- Dragonflies
- Ladybugs
- Birds/Hummingbirds
- Diseased or Sick Plants
- _____
- _____
- _____
- _____

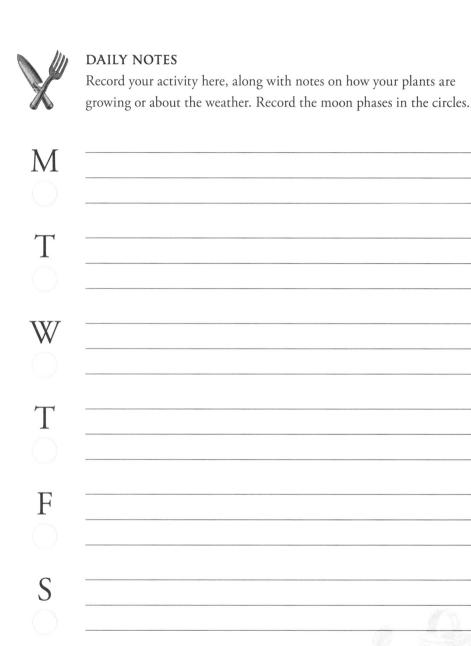

DAILY NOTES
Record your activity here, along with notes on how your plants are growing or about the weather. Record the moon phases in the circles.

M

T

W

T

F

S

S

FROM ___ / ___ / ___   TO ___ / ___ / ___

Weekly Log

ASTROLOGICAL NOTES
(E.g., Sun sign, Moon sign, astrological events.)

_____
_____
_____
_____
_____
_____
_____

	TEMPS _High/Low_	RAINFALL _Inches_
M	/	
T	/	
W	/	
T	/	
F	/	
S	/	
S	/	

TO-DO ITEMS
- Fertilize
- Harvest
- Weed
- Prune
- _____
- _____
- _____
- _____
- _____
- _____
- _____

OBSERVED
- Wildlife
- Bees/Other Pollinators
- Butterflies
- Dragonflies
- Ladybugs
- Birds/Hummingbirds
- Diseased or Sick Plants
- _____
- _____
- _____
- _____

DAILY NOTES

Record your activity here, along with notes on how your plants are growing or about the weather. Record the moon phases in the circles.

M

T

W

T

F

S

S

Weekly Log

ASTROLOGICAL NOTES
(E.g., Sun sign, Moon sign, astrological events.)

	TEMPS High/Low	RAINFALL Inches
M	/	
T	/	
W	/	
T	/	
F	/	
S	/	
S	/	

_____

_____

_____

_____

_____

_____

_____

TO-DO ITEMS

- Fertilize
- Harvest
- Weed
- Prune
- _____
- _____
- _____
- _____
- _____
- _____
- _____
- _____

OBSERVED

- Wildlife
- Bees/Other Pollinators
- Butterflies
- Dragonflies
- Ladybugs
- Birds/Hummingbirds
- Diseased or Sick Plants
- _____
- _____
- _____
- _____
- _____

DAILY NOTES

Record your activity here, along with notes on how your plants are growing or about the weather. Record the moon phases in the circles.

M ○

_____
_____
_____

T ○

_____
_____
_____

W ○

_____
_____
_____

T ○

_____
_____
_____

F ○

_____
_____
_____

S ○

_____
_____
_____

S ○

_____
_____
_____

Weekly Log

ASTROLOGICAL NOTES
(E.g., Sun sign, Moon sign, astrological events.)

_____

_____

_____

_____

_____

_____

_____

	TEMPS _High/Low_	RAINFALL _Inches_
M	/	
T	/	
W	/	
T	/	
F	/	
S	/	
S	/	

TO-DO ITEMS
- Fertilize
- Harvest
- Weed
- Prune
- _____
- _____
- _____
- _____
- _____
- _____
- _____

OBSERVED
- Wildlife
- Bees/Other Pollinators
- Butterflies
- Dragonflies
- Ladybugs
- Birds/Hummingbirds
- Diseased or Sick Plants
- _____
- _____
- _____
- _____

DAILY NOTES

Record your activity here, along with notes on how your plants are growing or about the weather. Record the moon phases in the circles.

M

T

W

T

F

S

S

Weekly Log

ASTROLOGICAL NOTES
(E.g., Sun sign, Moon sign, astrological events.)

	TEMPS High/Low	RAINFALL Inches
M	/	
T	/	
W	/	
T	/	
F	/	
S	/	
S	/	

TO-DO ITEMS

- Fertilize
- Harvest
- Weed
- Prune
- _____
- _____
- _____
- _____
- _____
- _____
- _____

OBSERVED

- Wildlife
- Bees/Other Pollinators
- Butterflies
- Dragonflies
- Ladybugs
- Birds/Hummingbirds
- Diseased or Sick Plants
- _____
- _____
- _____
- _____

DAILY NOTES

Record your activity here, along with notes on how your plants are growing or about the weather. Record the moon phases in the circles.

M

T

W

T

F

S

S

Weekly Log

ASTROLOGICAL NOTES
(E.g., Sun sign, Moon sign, astrological events.)

	TEMPS *High/Low*	RAINFALL *Inches*
M	/	
T	/	
W	/	
T	/	
F	/	
S	/	
S	/	

TO-DO ITEMS

- Fertilize
- Harvest
- Weed
- Prune
- _____
- _____
- _____
- _____
- _____
- _____
- _____

OBSERVED

- Wildlife
- Bees/Other Pollinators
- Butterflies
- Dragonflies
- Ladybugs
- Birds/Hummingbirds
- Diseased or Sick Plants
- _____
- _____
- _____
- _____

DAILY NOTES

Record your activity here, along with notes on how your plants are growing or about the weather. Record the moon phases in the circles.

M

T

W

T

F

S

S

Weekly Log

ASTROLOGICAL NOTES
(E.g., Sun sign, Moon sign, astrological events.)

	TEMPS	RAINFALL
	High/Low	*Inches*
M	/	
T	/	
W	/	
T	/	
F	/	
S	/	
S	/	

_____

_____

_____

_____

_____

_____

_____

TO-DO ITEMS

- Fertilize
- Harvest
- Weed
- Prune
- _____
- _____
- _____
- _____
- _____
- _____

OBSERVED

- Wildlife
- Bees/Other Pollinators
- Butterflies
- Dragonflies
- Ladybugs
- Birds/Hummingbirds
- Diseased or Sick Plants
- _____
- _____
- _____
- _____

DAILY NOTES

Record your activity here, along with notes on how your plants are growing or about the weather. Record the moon phases in the circles.

M

T

W

T

F

S

S

Weekly Log

ASTROLOGICAL NOTES
(E.g., Sun sign, Moon sign, astrological events.)

	TEMPS	RAINFALL
	High/Low	*Inches*
M	/	
T	/	
W	/	
T	/	
F	/	
S	/	
S	/	

TO-DO ITEMS

- Fertilize
- Harvest
- Weed
- Prune
-
-
-
-
-
-
-

OBSERVED

- Wildlife
- Bees/Other Pollinators
- Butterflies
- Dragonflies
- Ladybugs
- Birds/Hummingbirds
- Diseased or Sick Plants
-
-
-
-
-

DAILY NOTES

Record your activity here, along with notes on how your plants are growing or about the weather. Record the moon phases in the circles.

M ◯

T ◯

W ◯

T ◯

F ◯

S ◯

S ◯

Weekly Log

ASTROLOGICAL NOTES
(E.g., Sun sign, Moon sign, astrological events.)

_____

_____

_____

_____

_____

_____

_____

	TEMPS High/Low	RAINFALL Inches
M	/	
T	/	
W	/	
T	/	
F	/	
S	/	
S	/	

TO-DO ITEMS

- Fertilize
- Harvest
- Weed
- Prune
- _____
- _____
- _____
- _____
- _____
- _____
- _____
- _____

OBSERVED

- Wildlife
- Bees/Other Pollinators
- Butterflies
- Dragonflies
- Ladybugs
- Birds/Hummingbirds
- Diseased or Sick Plants
- _____
- _____
- _____
- _____
- _____

DAILY NOTES

Record your activity here, along with notes on how your plants are growing or about the weather. Record the moon phases in the circles.

M ○

T ○

W ○

T ○

F ○

S ○

S ○

Weekly Log

ASTROLOGICAL NOTES
(E.g., Sun sign, Moon sign, astrological events.)

	TEMPS *High/Low*	RAINFALL *Inches*
M	/	
T	/	
W	/	
T	/	
F	/	
S	/	
S	/	

TO-DO ITEMS

- Fertilize
- Harvest
- Weed
- Prune
-
-
-
-
-
-
-
-

OBSERVED

- Wildlife
- Bees/Other Pollinators
- Butterflies
- Dragonflies
- Ladybugs
- Birds/Hummingbirds
- Diseased or Sick Plants
-
-
-
-

DAILY NOTES

Record your activity here, along with notes on how your plants are growing or about the weather. Record the moon phases in the circles.

M

T

W

T

F

S

S

Weekly Log

ASTROLOGICAL NOTES
(E.g., Sun sign, Moon sign, astrological events.)

_____

_____

_____

_____

_____

_____

_____

	TEMPS High/Low	RAINFALL Inches
M	/	
T	/	
W	/	
T	/	
F	/	
S	/	
S	/	

TO-DO ITEMS

- Fertilize
- Harvest
- Weed
- Prune
- _____
- _____
- _____
- _____
- _____
- _____
- _____
- _____

OBSERVED

- Wildlife
- Bees/Other Pollinators
- Butterflies
- Dragonflies
- Ladybugs
- Birds/Hummingbirds
- Diseased or Sick Plants
- _____
- _____
- _____
- _____

DAILY NOTES
Record your activity here, along with notes on how your plants are growing or about the weather. Record the moon phases in the circles.

M

T

W

T

F

S

S

Weekly Log

ASTROLOGICAL NOTES
(E.g., Sun sign, Moon sign, astrological events.)

_____

_____

_____

_____

_____

_____

_____

	TEMPS High/Low	RAINFALL Inches
M	/	
T	/	
W	/	
T	/	
F	/	
S	/	
S	/	

TO-DO ITEMS

- Fertilize
- Harvest
- Weed
- Prune
- _____
- _____
- _____
- _____
- _____
- _____
- _____
- _____

OBSERVED

- Wildlife
- Bees/Other Pollinators
- Butterflies
- Dragonflies
- Ladybugs
- Birds/Hummingbirds
- Diseased or Sick Plants
- _____
- _____
- _____
- _____

DAILY NOTES
Record your activity here, along with notes on how your plants are growing or about the weather. Record the moon phases in the circles.

M ○ _____

T ○ _____

W ○ _____

T ○ _____

F ○ _____

S ○ _____

S ○ _____

Weekly Log

ASTROLOGICAL NOTES
(E.g., Sun sign, Moon sign, astrological events.)

_____

_____

_____

_____

_____

_____

_____

	TEMPS High/Low	RAINFALL Inches
M	/	
T	/	
W	/	
T	/	
F	/	
S	/	
S	/	

TO-DO ITEMS

- Fertilize
- Harvest
- Weed
- Prune
- _____
- _____
- _____
- _____
- _____
- _____
- _____
- _____

OBSERVED

- Wildlife
- Bees/Other Pollinators
- Butterflies
- Dragonflies
- Ladybugs
- Birds/Hummingbirds
- Diseased or Sick Plants
- _____
- _____
- _____
- _____

DAILY NOTES

Record your activity here, along with notes on how your plants are growing or about the weather. Record the moon phases in the circles.

M

T

W

T

F

S

S

Weekly Log

ASTROLOGICAL NOTES
(E.g., Sun sign, Moon sign, astrological events.)

_____

_____

_____

_____

_____

_____

_____

	TEMPS _High/Low_	RAINFALL _Inches_
M	/	
T	/	
W	/	
T	/	
F	/	
S	/	
S	/	

TO-DO ITEMS

- Fertilize
- Harvest
- Weed
- Prune
- _____
- _____
- _____
- _____
- _____
- _____
- _____

OBSERVED

- Wildlife
- Bees/Other Pollinators
- Butterflies
- Dragonflies
- Ladybugs
- Birds/Hummingbirds
- Diseased or Sick Plants
- _____
- _____
- _____
- _____

DAILY NOTES

Record your activity here, along with notes on how your plants are growing or about the weather. Record the moon phases in the circles.

M

T

W

T

F

S

S

Weekly Log

ASTROLOGICAL NOTES
(E.g., Sun sign, Moon sign, astrological events.)

_____

_____

_____

_____

_____

_____

_____

	TEMPS High/Low	RAINFALL Inches
M	/	
T	/	
W	/	
T	/	
F	/	
S	/	
S	/	

TO-DO ITEMS

- Fertilize
- Harvest
- Weed
- Prune
- _____
- _____
- _____
- _____
- _____
- _____
- _____
- _____

OBSERVED

- Wildlife
- Bees/Other Pollinators
- Butterflies
- Dragonflies
- Ladybugs
- Birds/Hummingbirds
- Diseased or Sick Plants
- _____
- _____
- _____
- _____
- _____

DAILY NOTES

Record your activity here, along with notes on how your plants are growing or about the weather. Record the moon phases in the circles.

M

T

W

T

F

S

S

Weekly Log

ASTROLOGICAL NOTES
(E.g., Sun sign, Moon sign, astrological events.)

_____

_____

_____

_____

_____

_____

_____

	TEMPS High/Low	RAINFALL Inches
M	/	
T	/	
W	/	
T	/	
F	/	
S	/	
S	/	

TO-DO ITEMS

- Fertilize
- Harvest
- Weed
- Prune
- _____
- _____
- _____
- _____
- _____
- _____
- _____

OBSERVED

- Wildlife
- Bees/Other Pollinators
- Butterflies
- Dragonflies
- Ladybugs
- Birds/Hummingbirds
- Diseased or Sick Plants
- _____
- _____
- _____
- _____

DAILY NOTES

Record your activity here, along with notes on how your plants are growing or about the weather. Record the moon phases in the circles.

M

T

W

T

F

S

S

Section Three

My Garden
Plants

Plant Compendium

COMMON NAME

_____

LATIN NAME

_____

DESCRIPTION

_____

_____

_____

_____

_____

_____

MAGICAL PROPERTIES   **MAGICAL CORRESPONDENCES/FOLKLORE**

_____   _____

_____   _____

_____   _____

_____   _____

MAGICAL NOTES Record spells or charms you used; magical elements that visited the garden.

PLANTING HISTORY

Task	Date	Notes
Started seeds:		
Germination:		
Transplanted:		
Bloom date:		
Harvest date:		

CULTURE NOTES Make notes about the ideal conditions for this plant.

USDA zone	3A/B	4A/B	5A/B	6A/B	7A/B	8A/B	9A/B	10A/B

Soil type   Sandy   Loamy   Clay   Mixed   Potting mix

Water needs   Low   Medium   High   Aquatic   Air

Sunlight   Shade   Moderate   Full sun   Direct   Indirect

FERTILIZER SCHEDULE

Date	Type	Frequency

PRUNING/TRIMMING SCHEDULE

Date	Type	Frequency

PESTS

Date	Type	Treatment

DISEASES

Date	Type	Treatment

 *Plant Compendium*

COMMON NAME

_____

LATIN NAME

_____

DESCRIPTION

_____

_____

_____

_____

_____

Draw the plant, paste a picture, or paste a leaf press.

MAGICAL PROPERTIES   **MAGICAL CORRESPONDENCES/FOLKLORE**

_____   _____

_____   _____

                                 _____

_____   _____

MAGICAL NOTES   Record spells or charms you used; magical elements that visited the garden.

PLANTING HISTORY

Task	Date	Notes
Started seeds:		
Germination:		
Transplanted:		
Bloom date:		
Harvest date:		

CULTURE NOTES Make notes about the ideal conditions for this plant.

USDA zone	3A/B	4A/B	5A/B	6A/B	7A/B	8A/B	9A/B	10A/B
Soil type	Sandy	Loamy	Clay	Mixed	Potting mix			
Water needs	Low	Medium	High	Aquatic	Air			
Sunlight	Shade	Moderate	Full sun	Direct	Indirect			

FERTILIZER SCHEDULE

Date	*Type*	*Frequency*

PRUNING/TRIMMING SCHEDULE

Date	*Type*	*Frequency*

PESTS

Date	*Type*	*Treatment*

DISEASES

Date	*Type*	*Treatment*

Plant Compendium

COMMON NAME

_____

LATIN NAME

_____

DESCRIPTION

_____

_____

_____

_____

_____

_____

Draw the plant, paste a picture, or paste a leaf press

MAGICAL PROPERTIES

_____

_____

_____

_____

MAGICAL CORRESPONDENCES/FOLKLORE

_____

_____

_____

_____

MAGICAL NOTES Record spells or charms you used; magical elements that visited the garden.

PLANTING HISTORY

Task	Date	Notes
Started seeds:		
Germination:		
Transplanted:		
Bloom date:		
Harvest date:		

CULTURE NOTES Make notes about the ideal conditions for this plant.

USDA zone	3A/B	4A/B	5A/B	6A/B	7A/B	8A/B	9A/B	10A/B
Soil type	Sandy	Loamy		Clay		Mixed	Potting mix	
Water needs	Low	Medium		High		Aquatic	Air	
Sunlight	Shade	Moderate		Full sun		Direct	Indirect	

FERTILIZER SCHEDULE

Date	Type	Frequency

PRUNING/TRIMMING SCHEDULE

Date	Type	Frequency

PESTS

Date	Type	Treatment

DISEASES

Date	Type	Treatment

Plant Compendium

COMMON NAME

_____

LATIN NAME

_____

DESCRIPTION

_____

_____

_____

_____

_____

_____

Draw the plant, paste a picture, or paste a leaf press

MAGICAL PROPERTIES

_____

_____

_____

_____

MAGICAL CORRESPONDENCES/FOLKLORE

_____

_____

_____

_____

MAGICAL NOTES Record spells or charms you used; magical elements that visited the garden.

PLANTING HISTORY

Task	Date	Notes
Started seeds:		
Germination:		
Transplanted:		
Bloom date:		
Harvest date:		

CULTURE NOTES   Make notes about the ideal conditions for this plant.

USDA zone	3A/B	4A/B	5A/B	6A/B	7A/B	8A/B	9A/B	10A/B
Soil type	Sandy	Loamy	Clay	Mixed	Potting mix			
Water needs	Low	Medium	High	Aquatic	Air			
Sunlight	Shade	Moderate	Full sun	Direct	Indirect			

FERTILIZER SCHEDULE

Date	Type	Frequency

PRUNING/TRIMMING SCHEDULE

Date	Type	Frequency

PESTS

Date	Type	Treatment

DISEASES

Date	Type	Treatment

Plant Compendium

COMMON NAME

_____

LATIN NAME

_____

DESCRIPTION

_____

_____

_____

_____

_____

_____

Draw the plant, paste a picture, or paste a leaf press

MAGICAL PROPERTIES

_____

_____

_____

_____

MAGICAL CORRESPONDENCES/FOLKLORE

_____

_____

_____

_____

MAGICAL NOTES Record spells or charms you used; magical elements that visited the garden.

PLANTING HISTORY

Task	Date	Notes
Started seeds:		
Germination:		
Transplanted:		
Bloom date:		
Harvest date:		

CULTURE NOTES Make notes about the ideal conditions for this plant.

USDA zone	3A/B	4A/B	5A/B	6A/B	7A/B	8A/B	9A/B	10A/B
Soil type	Sandy	Loamy	Clay	Mixed	Potting mix			
Water needs	Low	Medium	High	Aquatic	Air			
Sunlight	Shade	Moderate	Full sun	Direct	Indirect			

FERTILIZER SCHEDULE

Date	Type	Frequency

PRUNING/TRIMMING SCHEDULE

Date	Type	Frequency

PESTS

Date	Type	Treatment

DISEASES

Date	Type	Treatment

Plant Compendium

COMMON NAME

_____

LATIN NAME

_____

DESCRIPTION

_____

_____

_____

_____

_____

_____

Draw the plant, paste a picture, or create a leaf press

MAGICAL PROPERTIES

_____

_____

_____

_____

MAGICAL CORRESPONDENCES/FOLKLORE

_____

_____

_____

_____

MAGICAL NOTES   Record spells or charms you used; magical elements that visited the garden.

PLANTING HISTORY

Task	Date	Notes
Started seeds:		
Germination:		
Transplanted:		
Bloom date:		
Harvest date:		

CULTURE NOTES Make notes about the ideal conditions for this plant.

USDA zone	3A/B	4A/B	5A/B	6A/B	7A/B	8A/B	9A/B	10A/B
Soil type	Sandy	Loamy	Clay		Mixed		Potting mix	
Water needs	Low	Medium	High		Aquatic		Air	
Sunlight	Shade	Moderate	Full sun		Direct		Indirect	

FERTILIZER SCHEDULE

Date	Type	Frequency

PRUNING/TRIMMING SCHEDULE

Date	Type	Frequency

PESTS

Date	Type	Treatment

DISEASES

Date	Type	Treatment

Plant Compendium

COMMON NAME

_____

LATIN NAME

_____

DESCRIPTION

_____

_____

_____

_____

_____

_____

MAGICAL PROPERTIES

_____

_____

_____

_____

MAGICAL CORRESPONDENCES/FOLKLORE

_____

_____

_____

_____

MAGICAL NOTES   Record spells or charms you used; magical elements that visited the garden.

PLANTING HISTORY

Task	Date	Notes
Started seeds:		
Germination:		
Transplanted:		
Bloom date:		
Harvest date:		

CULTURE NOTES Make notes about the ideal conditions for this plant.

USDA zone	3A/B	4A/B	5A/B	6A/B	7A/B	8A/B	9A/B	10A/B
Soil type	Sandy	Loamy	Clay	Mixed	Potting mix		
Water needs	Low	Medium	High	Aquatic	Air		
Sunlight	Shade	Moderate	Full sun	Direct	Indirect		

FERTILIZER SCHEDULE

Date	Type	Frequency

PRUNING/TRIMMING SCHEDULE

Date	Type	Frequency

PESTS

Date	Type	Treatment

DISEASES

Date	Type	Treatment

COMMON NAME

_____

LATIN NAME

_____

DESCRIPTION

_____

_____

_____

_____

_____

_____

Draw the plant, paste a picture, or paste a leaf press

MAGICAL PROPERTIES

_____

_____

_____

_____

MAGICAL CORRESPONDENCES/FOLKLORE

_____

_____

_____

_____

MAGICAL NOTES Record spells or charms you used; magical elements that visited the garden.

PLANTING HISTORY

Task	Date	Notes
Started seeds:		
Germination:		
Transplanted:		
Bloom date:		
Harvest date:		

CULTURE NOTES Make notes about the ideal conditions for this plant.

USDA zone	3A/B	4A/B	5A/B	6A/B	7A/B	8A/B	9A/B	10A/B
Soil type	Sandy	Loamy	Clay	Mixed	Potting mix
Water needs	Low	Medium	High	Aquatic	Air
Sunlight	Shade	Moderate	Full sun	Direct	Indirect

FERTILIZER SCHEDULE

Date	Type	Frequency

PRUNING/TRIMMING SCHEDULE

Date	Type	Frequency

PESTS

Date	Type	Treatment

DISEASES

Date	Type	Treatment

Plant Compendium

COMMON NAME

_____

LATIN NAME

_____

DESCRIPTION

_____

_____

_____

_____

_____

Draw the plant, paste a picture, or paste a leaf press

MAGICAL PROPERTIES

_____

_____

_____

_____

MAGICAL CORRESPONDENCES/FOLKLORE

_____

_____

_____

_____

MAGICAL NOTES Record spells or charms you used; magical elements that visited the garden.

PLANTING HISTORY

Task	Date	Notes
Started seeds:		
Germination:		
Transplanted:		
Bloom date:		
Harvest date:		

CULTURE NOTES Make notes about the ideal conditions for this plant.

USDA zone	3A/B	4A/B	5A/B	6A/B	7A/B	8A/B	9A/B	10A/B
Soil type	Sandy	Loamy	Clay		Mixed		Potting mix	
Water needs	Low	Medium	High		Aquatic		Air	
Sunlight	Shade	Moderate	Full sun		Direct		Indirect	

FERTILIZER SCHEDULE

Date	Type	Frequency

PRUNING/TRIMMING SCHEDULE

Date	Type	Frequency

PESTS

Date	Type	Treatment

DISEASES

Date	Type	Treatment

Plant Compendium

COMMON NAME

_____

LATIN NAME

_____

DESCRIPTION

_____

_____

_____

_____

_____

_____

MAGICAL PROPERTIES

_____

_____

_____

_____

MAGICAL CORRESPONDENCES/FOLKLORE

_____

_____

_____

_____

MAGICAL NOTES Record spells or charms you used; magical elements that visited the garden.

PLANTING HISTORY

Task	Date	Notes
Started seeds:		
Germination:		
Transplanted:		
Bloom date:		
Harvest date:		

CULTURE NOTES Make notes about the ideal conditions for this plant.

USDA zone	3A/B	4A/B	5A/B	6A/B	7A/B	8A/B	9A/B	10A/B

Soil type   Sandy   Loamy   Clay   Mixed   Potting mix

Water needs   Low   Medium   High   Aquatic   Air

Sunlight   Shade   Moderate   Full sun   Direct   Indirect

FERTILIZER SCHEDULE

Date	*Type*	*Frequency*

PRUNING/TRIMMING SCHEDULE

Date	*Type*	*Frequency*

PESTS

Date	*Type*	*Treatment*

DISEASES

Date	*Type*	*Treatment*

 # *Plant Compendium*

COMMON NAME

_____

LATIN NAME

_____

DESCRIPTION

_____
_____
_____
_____
_____
_____

Draw the plant, paste a picture, or paste a leaf press.

MAGICAL PROPERTIES   **MAGICAL CORRESPONDENCES/FOLKLORE**

_____   _____
_____   _____
_____   _____
_____   _____

MAGICAL NOTES   Record spells or charms you used; magical elements that visited the garden.

PLANTING HISTORY

Task	Date	Notes
Started seeds:		
Germination:		
Transplanted:		
Bloom date:		
Harvest date:		

CULTURE NOTES Make notes about the ideal conditions for this plant.

USDA zone	3A/B	4A/B	5A/B	6A/B	7A/B	8A/B	9A/B	10A/B
Soil type	Sandy	Loamy	Clay	Mixed	Potting mix			
Water needs	Low	Medium	High	Aquatic	Air			
Sunlight	Shade	Moderate	Full sun	Direct	Indirect			

FERTILIZER SCHEDULE

Date	*Type*	*Frequency*

PRUNING/TRIMMING SCHEDULE

Date	*Type*	*Frequency*

PESTS

Date	*Type*	*Treatment*

DISEASES

Date	*Type*	*Treatment*

Plant Compendium

COMMON NAME

_____

LATIN NAME

_____

DESCRIPTION

_____

_____

_____

_____

_____

_____

Draw the plant, paste a picture, or paste a leaf press

MAGICAL PROPERTIES   MAGICAL CORRESPONDENCES/FOLKLORE

_____   _____

_____   _____

_____   _____

_____   _____

MAGICAL NOTES   Record spells or charms you used; magical elements that visited the garden.

PLANTING HISTORY

Task	Date	Notes
Started seeds:		
Germination:		
Transplanted:		
Bloom date:		
Harvest date:		

CULTURE NOTES Make notes about the ideal conditions for this plant.

USDA zone	3A/B	4A/B	5A/B	6A/B	7A/B	8A/B	9A/B	10A/B
Soil type	Sandy	Loamy	Clay	Mixed	Potting mix			
Water needs	Low	Medium	High	Aquatic	Air			
Sunlight	Shade	Moderate	Full sun	Direct	Indirect			

FERTILIZER SCHEDULE

Date	*Type*	*Frequency*

PRUNING/TRIMMING SCHEDULE

Date	*Type*	*Frequency*

PESTS

Date	*Type*	*Treatment*

DISEASES

Date	*Type*	*Treatment*

Plant Compendium

COMMON NAME

_____

LATIN NAME

_____

DESCRIPTION

_____

_____

_____

_____

_____

_____

Draw the plant, paste a picture, or paste a leaf press

MAGICAL PROPERTIES

_____

_____

_____

_____

MAGICAL CORRESPONDENCES/FOLKLORE

_____

_____

_____

_____

MAGICAL NOTES Record spells or charms you used; magical elements that visited the garden.

PLANTING HISTORY

Task	Date	Notes
Started seeds:		
Germination:		
Transplanted:		
Bloom date:		
Harvest date:		

CULTURE NOTES Make notes about the ideal conditions for this plant.

USDA zone	3A/B	4A/B	5A/B	6A/B	7A/B	8A/B	9A/B	10A/B
Soil type	Sandy	Loamy	Clay	Mixed	Potting mix
Water needs	Low	Medium	High	Aquatic	Air
Sunlight	Shade	Moderate	Full sun	Direct	Indirect

FERTILIZER SCHEDULE

Date	Type	Frequency

PRUNING/TRIMMING SCHEDULE

Date	Type	Frequency

PESTS

Date	Type	Treatment

DISEASES

Date	Type	Treatment

COMMON NAME

LATIN NAME

DESCRIPTION

Draw the plant, paste a picture, or paste a leaf press.

MAGICAL PROPERTIES

MAGICAL CORRESPONDENCES/FOLKLORE

MAGICAL NOTES Record spells or charms you used; magical elements that visited the garden.

PLANTING HISTORY

Task	Date	Notes
Started seeds:		
Germination:		
Transplanted:		
Bloom date:		
Harvest date:		

CULTURE NOTES   Make notes about the ideal conditions for this plant.

USDA zone	3A/B	4A/B	5A/B	6A/B	7A/B	8A/B	9A/B	10A/B
Soil type	Sandy	Loamy	Clay	Mixed	Potting mix
Water needs	Low	Medium	High	Aquatic	Air
Sunlight	Shade	Moderate	Full sun	Direct	Indirect

FERTILIZER SCHEDULE

Date	Type	Frequency

PRUNING/TRIMMING SCHEDULE

Date	Type	Frequency

PESTS

Date	Type	Treatment

DISEASES

Date	Type	Treatment

Plant Compendium

COMMON NAME

LATIN NAME

DESCRIPTION

MAGICAL PROPERTIES   **MAGICAL CORRESPONDENCES/FOLKLORE**

MAGICAL NOTES   Record spells or charms you used; magical elements that visited the garden.

PLANTING HISTORY

Task	Date	Notes
Started seeds:		
Germination:		
Transplanted:		
Bloom date:		
Harvest date:		

CULTURE NOTES   Make notes about the ideal conditions for this plant.

USDA zone   3A/B   4A/B   5A/B   6A/B   7A/B   8A/B   9A/B   10A/B

Soil type   Sandy   Loamy   Clay   Mixed   Potting mix

Water needs   Low   Medium   High   Aquatic   Air

Sunlight   Shade   Moderate   Full sun   Direct   Indirect

FERTILIZER SCHEDULE

Date	Type	Frequency

PRUNING/TRIMMING SCHEDULE

Date	Type	Frequency

PESTS

Date	Type	Treatment

DISEASES

Date	Type	Treatment

Plant Compendium

COMMON NAME

_____

LATIN NAME

_____

DESCRIPTION

_____

_____

_____

_____

_____

_____

Draw the plant, paste a picture, or paste a leaf press

MAGICAL PROPERTIES

_____

_____

_____

_____

MAGICAL CORRESPONDENCES/FOLKLORE

_____

_____

_____

_____

MAGICAL NOTES Record spells or charms you used; magical elements that visited the garden.

PLANTING HISTORY

Task	Date	Notes
Started seeds:		
Germination:		
Transplanted:		
Bloom date:		
Harvest date:		

CULTURE NOTES Make notes about the ideal conditions for this plant.

USDA zone	3A/B	4A/B	5A/B	6A/B	7A/B	8A/B	9A/B	10A/B
Soil type	Sandy	Loamy	Clay	Mixed	Potting mix
Water needs	Low	Medium	High	Aquatic	Air
Sunlight	Shade	Moderate	Full sun	Direct	Indirect

FERTILIZER SCHEDULE

Date	Type	Frequency

PRUNING/TRIMMING SCHEDULE

Date	Type	Frequency

PESTS

Date	Type	Treatment

DISEASES

Date	Type	Treatment

Plant Compendium

COMMON NAME

_____

LATIN NAME

_____

DESCRIPTION

_____

_____

_____

_____

_____

Draw the plant, paste a picture, or paste a leaf scan.

MAGICAL PROPERTIES

_____

_____

_____

_____

MAGICAL CORRESPONDENCES/FOLKLORE

_____

_____

_____

_____

MAGICAL NOTES Record spells or charms you used; magical elements that visited the garden.

PLANTING HISTORY

Task   *Date*   *Notes*

Started seeds:

Germination:

Transplanted:

Bloom date:

Harvest date:

CULTURE NOTES Make notes about the ideal conditions for this plant.

USDA zone   3A/B   4A/B   5A/B   6A/B   7A/B   8A/B   9A/B   10A/B

Soil type   Sandy   Loamy   Clay   Mixed   Potting mix

Water needs   Low   Medium   High   Aquatic   Air

Sunlight   Shade   Moderate   Full sun   Direct   Indirect

FERTILIZER SCHEDULE

Date   *Type*   *Frequency*

PRUNING/TRIMMING SCHEDULE

Date   *Type*   *Frequency*

PESTS

Date   *Type*   *Treatment*

DISEASES

Date   *Type*   *Treatment*

 # Plant Compendium

COMMON NAME

_____

LATIN NAME

_____

DESCRIPTION

_____
_____
_____
_____
_____
_____

Draw the plant, paste a picture, or paste a leaf press.

MAGICAL PROPERTIES

_____
_____
_____
_____

MAGICAL CORRESPONDENCES/FOLKLORE

_____
_____
_____
_____

MAGICAL NOTES Record spells or charms you used; magical elements that visited the garden.

PLANTING HISTORY

Task	Date	Notes
Started seeds:		
Germination:		
Transplanted:		
Bloom date:		
Harvest date:		

CULTURE NOTES Make notes about the ideal conditions for this plant.

USDA zone	3A/B	4A/B	5A/B	6A/B	7A/B	8A/B	9A/B	10A/B
Soil type	Sandy	Loamy	Clay	Mixed	Potting mix
Water needs	Low	Medium	High	Aquatic	Air
Sunlight	Shade	Moderate	Full sun	Direct	Indirect

FERTILIZER SCHEDULE

Date	Type	Frequency

PRUNING/TRIMMING SCHEDULE

Date	Type	Frequency

PESTS

Date	Type	Treatment

DISEASES

Date	Type	Treatment

Plant Compendium

COMMON NAME

_____

LATIN NAME

_____

DESCRIPTION

_____

_____

_____

_____

_____

_____

Draw the plant, paste a picture, or paste a leaf press

MAGICAL PROPERTIES

_____

_____

_____

_____

MAGICAL CORRESPONDENCES/FOLKLORE

_____

_____

_____

_____

MAGICAL NOTES Record spells or charms you used; magical elements that visited the garden.

PLANTING HISTORY

Task	Date	Notes
Started seeds:		
Germination:		
Transplanted:		
Bloom date:		
Harvest date:		

CULTURE NOTES Make notes about the ideal conditions for this plant.

USDA zone	3A/B	4A/B	5A/B	6A/B	7A/B	8A/B	9A/B	10A/B

Soil type   Sandy   Loamy   Clay   Mixed   Potting mix

Water needs   Low   Medium   High   Aquatic   Air

Sunlight   Shade   Moderate   Full sun   Direct   Indirect

FERTILIZER SCHEDULE

Date	*Type*	*Frequency*

PRUNING/TRIMMING SCHEDULE

Date	*Type*	*Frequency*

PESTS

Date	*Type*	*Treatment*

DISEASES

Date	*Type*	*Treatment*

Plant Compendium

COMMON NAME

_____

LATIN NAME

_____

DESCRIPTION

_____
_____
_____
_____
_____
_____

Draw the plant, paste a picture, or paste a leaf press.

MAGICAL PROPERTIES

_____
_____
_____
_____

MAGICAL CORRESPONDENCES/FOLKLORE

_____
_____
_____
_____

MAGICAL NOTES   Record spells or charms you used; magical elements that visited the garden.

PLANTING HISTORY

Task	Date	Notes
Started seeds:		
Germination:		
Transplanted:		
Bloom date:		
Harvest date:		

CULTURE NOTES Make notes about the ideal conditions for this plant.

USDA zone	3A/B	4A/B	5A/B	6A/B	7A/B	8A/B	9A/B 10A/B
Soil type	Sandy	Loamy	Clay	Mixed	Potting mix		
Water needs	Low	Medium	High	Aquatic	Air		
Sunlight	Shade	Moderate	Full sun	Direct	Indirect		

FERTILIZER SCHEDULE

Date	Type	Frequency

PRUNING/TRIMMING SCHEDULE

Date	Type	Frequency

PESTS

Date	Type	Treatment

DISEASES

Date	Type	Treatment

 # Plant Compendium

COMMON NAME

_____

LATIN NAME

_____

DESCRIPTION

_____

_____

_____

_____

_____

_____

MAGICAL PROPERTIES

_____

_____

_____

_____

MAGICAL CORRESPONDENCES/FOLKLORE

_____

_____

_____

_____

MAGICAL NOTES Record spells or charms you used; magical elements that visited the garden.

PLANTING HISTORY

Task	Date	Notes
Started seeds:		
Germination:		
Transplanted:		
Bloom date:		
Harvest date:		

CULTURE NOTES Make notes about the ideal conditions for this plant.

USDA zone	3A/B	4A/B	5A/B	6A/B	7A/B	8A/B	9A/B	10A/B
Soil type	Sandy	Loamy	Clay	Mixed	Potting mix
Water needs	Low	Medium	High	Aquatic	Air
Sunlight	Shade	Moderate	Full sun	Direct	Indirect

FERTILIZER SCHEDULE

Date	Type	Frequency

PRUNING/TRIMMING SCHEDULE

Date	Type	Frequency

PESTS

Date	Type	Treatment

DISEASES

Date	Type	Treatment

Plant Compendium

COMMON NAME

_____

LATIN NAME

_____

DESCRIPTION

_____

_____

_____

_____

_____

_____

Draw the plant, paste a picture, or paste a leaf press

MAGICAL PROPERTIES

_____

_____

_____

_____

MAGICAL CORRESPONDENCES/FOLKLORE

_____

_____

_____

_____

MAGICAL NOTES   Record spells or charms you used; magical elements that visited the garden.

PLANTING HISTORY

Task	Date	Notes
Started seeds:		
Germination:		
Transplanted:		
Bloom date:		
Harvest date:		

CULTURE NOTES   Make notes about the ideal conditions for this plant.

USDA zone	3A/B	4A/B	5A/B	6A/B	7A/B	8A/B	9A/B	10A/B
Soil type	Sandy	Loamy		Clay		Mixed		Potting mix
Water needs	Low	Medium		High		Aquatic	Air	
Sunlight	Shade	Moderate		Full sun		Direct	Indirect	

FERTILIZER SCHEDULE

Date	Type	Frequency

PRUNING/TRIMMING SCHEDULE

Date	Type	Frequency

PESTS

Date	Type	Treatment

DISEASES

Date	Type	Treatment

Plant Compendium

COMMON NAME

_____

LATIN NAME

_____

DESCRIPTION

_____

_____

_____

_____

_____

_____

Draw the plant, paste a picture, or paste a leaf press

MAGICAL PROPERTIES

_____

_____

_____

_____

MAGICAL CORRESPONDENCES/FOLKLORE

_____

_____

_____

_____

MAGICAL NOTES   Record spells or charms you used; magical elements that visited the garden.

PLANTING HISTORY

Task	Date	Notes
Started seeds:		
Germination:		
Transplanted:		
Bloom date:		
Harvest date:		

CULTURE NOTES Make notes about the ideal conditions for this plant.

USDA zone	3A/B	4A/B	5A/B	6A/B	7A/B	8A/B	9A/B	10A/B
Soil type	Sandy	Loamy	Clay		Mixed	Potting mix		
Water needs	Low	Medium	High	Aquatic	Air			
Sunlight	Shade	Moderate	Full sun	Direct	Indirect			

FERTILIZER SCHEDULE

Date	Type	Frequency

PRUNING/TRIMMING SCHEDULE

Date	Type	Frequency

PESTS

Date	Type	Treatment

DISEASES

Date	Type	Treatment

Plant Compendium

COMMON NAME

LATIN NAME

DESCRIPTION

Draw the plant, paste a picture, or paste a leaf press.

MAGICAL PROPERTIES **MAGICAL CORRESPONDENCES/FOLKLORE**

MAGICAL NOTES Record spells or charms you used; magical elements that visited the garden.

PLANTING HISTORY

Task	Date	Notes
Started seeds:		
Germination:		
Transplanted:		
Bloom date:		
Harvest date:		

CULTURE NOTES   Make notes about the ideal conditions for this plant.

USDA zone	3A/B	4A/B	5A/B	6A/B	7A/B	8A/B	9A/B	10A/B
Soil type	Sandy	Loamy		Clay		Mixed		Potting mix
Water needs	Low	Medium		High		Aquatic	Air	
Sunlight	Shade	Moderate		Full sun		Direct	Indirect	

FERTILIZER SCHEDULE

Date	*Type*	*Frequency*

PRUNING/TRIMMING SCHEDULE

Date	*Type*	*Frequency*

PESTS

Date	*Type*	*Treatment*

DISEASES

Date	*Type*	*Treatment*

Plant Compendium

COMMON NAME

_____

LATIN NAME

_____

DESCRIPTION

_____

_____

_____

_____

_____

_____

Draw the plant, paste a picture, or paste a leaf press.

MAGICAL PROPERTIES

_____

_____

_____

_____

MAGICAL CORRESPONDENCES/FOLKLORE

_____

_____

_____

_____

MAGICAL NOTES Record spells or charms you used; magical elements that visited the garden.

PLANTING HISTORY

Task	Date	Notes
Started seeds:		
Germination:		
Transplanted:		
Bloom date:		
Harvest date:		

CULTURE NOTES Make notes about the ideal conditions for this plant.

USDA zone	3A/B	4A/B	5A/B	6A/B	7A/B	8A/B	9A/B	10A/B
Soil type	Sandy	Loamy	Clay	Mixed	Potting mix
Water needs	Low	Medium	High	Aquatic	Air
Sunlight	Shade	Moderate	Full sun	Direct	Indirect

FERTILIZER SCHEDULE

Date	Type	Frequency

PRUNING/TRIMMING SCHEDULE

Date	Type	Frequency

PESTS

Date	Type	Treatment

DISEASES

Date	Type	Treatment

Plant Compendium

COMMON NAME

LATIN NAME

DESCRIPTION

MAGICAL PROPERTIES   **MAGICAL CORRESPONDENCES/FOLKLORE**

MAGICAL NOTES Record spells or charms you used; magical elements that visited the garden.

PLANTING HISTORY

Task	Date	Notes
Started seeds:		
Germination:		
Transplanted:		
Bloom date:		
Harvest date:		

CULTURE NOTES Make notes about the ideal conditions for this plant.

USDA zone	3A/B	4A/B	5A/B	6A/B	7A/B	8A/B	9A/B	10A/B
Soil type	Sandy	Loamy		Clay		Mixed		Potting mix
Water needs	Low	Medium		High		Aquatic	Air	
Sunlight	Shade	Moderate		Full sun		Direct		Indirect

FERTILIZER SCHEDULE

Date	Type	Frequency

PRUNING/TRIMMING SCHEDULE

Date	Type	Frequency

PESTS

Date	Type	Treatment

DISEASES

Date	Type	Treatment

COMMON NAME

_____

LATIN NAME

_____

DESCRIPTION

_____

_____

_____

_____

_____

Draw the plant, paste a picture, or paste a leaf press.

MAGICAL PROPERTIES

_____

_____

_____

_____

MAGICAL CORRESPONDENCES/FOLKLORE

_____

_____

_____

MAGICAL NOTES Record spells or charms you used; magical elements that visited the garden.

PLANTING HISTORY

Task	Date	Notes
Started seeds:		
Germination:		
Transplanted:		
Bloom date:		
Harvest date:		

CULTURE NOTES Make notes about the ideal conditions for this plant.

USDA zone	3A/B	4A/B	5A/B	6A/B	7A/B	8A/B	9A/B	10A/B
Soil type	Sandy	Loamy	Clay	Mixed	Potting mix
Water needs	Low	Medium	High	Aquatic	Air
Sunlight	Shade	Moderate	Full sun	Direct	Indirect

FERTILIZER SCHEDULE

Date	Type	Frequency

PRUNING/TRIMMING SCHEDULE

Date	Type	Frequency

PESTS

Date	Type	Treatment

DISEASES

Date	Type	Treatment

Plant Compendium

COMMON NAME

_____

LATIN NAME

_____

DESCRIPTION

_____
_____
_____
_____
_____
_____

Draw the plant, paste a picture, or paste a leaf press.

MAGICAL PROPERTIES

_____
_____
_____

MAGICAL CORRESPONDENCES/FOLKLORE

_____
_____
_____
_____

MAGICAL NOTES Record spells or charms you used; magical elements that visited the garden.

PLANTING HISTORY

Task	Date	Notes
Started seeds:		
Germination:		
Transplanted:		
Bloom date:		
Harvest date:		

CULTURE NOTES   Make notes about the ideal conditions for this plant.

USDA zone	3A/B	4A/B	5A/B	6A/B	7A/B	8A/B	9A/B	10A/B
Soil type	Sandy	Loamy		Clay		Mixed		Potting mix
Water needs	Low	Medium		High		Aquatic	Air	
Sunlight	Shade	Moderate		Full sun		Direct	Indirect	

FERTILIZER SCHEDULE

Date	*Type*	*Frequency*

PRUNING/TRIMMING SCHEDULE

Date	*Type*	*Frequency*

PESTS

Date	*Type*	*Treatment*

DISEASES

Date	*Type*	*Treatment*

Plant Compendium

COMMON NAME

_____

LATIN NAME

_____

DESCRIPTION

_____

_____

_____

_____

_____

_____

Draw the plant, paste a picture, or paste a leaf press.

MAGICAL PROPERTIES

_____

_____

_____

_____

MAGICAL CORRESPONDENCES/FOLKLORE

_____

_____

_____

_____

MAGICAL NOTES Record spells or charms you used; magical elements that visited the garden.

PLANTING HISTORY

Task	Date	Notes
Started seeds:		
Germination:		
Transplanted:		
Bloom date:		
Harvest date:		

CULTURE NOTES Make notes about the ideal conditions for this plant.

USDA zone	3A/B	4A/B	5A/B	6A/B	7A/B	8A/B	9A/B	10A/B
Soil type	Sandy	Loamy		Clay		Mixed		Potting mix
Water needs	Low	Medium		High		Aquatic		Air
Sunlight	Shade	Moderate		Full sun		Direct		Indirect

FERTILIZER SCHEDULE

Date	Type	Frequency

PRUNING/TRIMMING SCHEDULE

Date	Type	Frequency

PESTS

Date	Type	Treatment

DISEASES

Date	Type	Treatment

Plant Compendium

COMMON NAME

_____

LATIN NAME

_____

DESCRIPTION

_____

_____

_____

_____

_____

_____

Draw the plant, paste a picture, or paste a leaf press.

MAGICAL PROPERTIES

_____

_____

_____

_____

MAGICAL CORRESPONDENCES/FOLKLORE

_____

_____

_____

_____

MAGICAL NOTES Record spells or charms you used; magical elements that visited the garden.

PLANTING HISTORY

Task	Date	Notes
Started seeds:		
Germination:		
Transplanted:		
Bloom date:		
Harvest date:		

CULTURE NOTES Make notes about the ideal conditions for this plant.

USDA zone	3A/B	4A/B	5A/B	6A/B	7A/B	8A/B	9A/B	10A/B
Soil type	Sandy	Loamy	Clay	Mixed	Potting mix			
Water needs	Low	Medium	High	Aquatic	Air			
Sunlight	Shade	Moderate	Full sun	Direct	Indirect			

FERTILIZER SCHEDULE

Date	Type	Frequency

PRUNING/TRIMMING SCHEDULE

Date	Type	Frequency

PESTS

Date	Type	Treatment

DISEASES

Date	Type	Treatment

Plant Compendium

COMMON NAME

_____

LATIN NAME

_____

DESCRIPTION

_____

_____

_____

_____

_____

_____

Draw the plant, paste a picture, or paste a leaf press

MAGICAL PROPERTIES   **MAGICAL CORRESPONDENCES/FOLKLORE**

_____   _____

_____   _____

_____   _____

_____   _____

MAGICAL NOTES Record spells or charms you used; magical elements that visited the garden.

194

PLANTING HISTORY

Task	Date	Notes
Started seeds:		
Germination:		
Transplanted:		
Bloom date:		
Harvest date:		

CULTURE NOTES Make notes about the ideal conditions for this plant.

USDA zone	3A/B	4A/B	5A/B	6A/B	7A/B	8A/B	9A/B	10A/B
Soil type	Sandy	Loamy	Clay	Mixed	Potting mix
Water needs	Low	Medium	High	Aquatic	Air
Sunlight	Shade	Moderate	Full sun	Direct	Indirect

FERTILIZER SCHEDULE

Date	Type	Frequency

PRUNING/TRIMMING SCHEDULE

Date	Type	Frequency

PESTS

Date	Type	Treatment

DISEASES

Date	Type	Treatment

 # Plant Compendium

COMMON NAME

_____

LATIN NAME

_____

DESCRIPTION

_____

_____

_____

_____

_____

_____

Draw the plant, paste a picture, or paste a leaf press.

MAGICAL PROPERTIES

_____

_____

_____

_____

MAGICAL CORRESPONDENCES/FOLKLORE

_____

_____

_____

_____

MAGICAL NOTES Record spells or charms you used; magical elements that visited the garden.

PLANTING HISTORY

Task	Date	Notes
Started seeds:		
Germination:		
Transplanted:		
Bloom date:		
Harvest date:		

CULTURE NOTES Make notes about the ideal conditions for this plant.

USDA zone	3A/B	4A/B	5A/B	6A/B	7A/B	8A/B	9A/B	10A/B
Soil type	Sandy	Loamy		Clay		Mixed	Potting mix	
Water needs	Low	Medium		High		Aquatic	Air	
Sunlight	Shade	Moderate		Full sun		Direct	Indirect	

FERTILIZER SCHEDULE

Date	Type	Frequency

PRUNING/TRIMMING SCHEDULE

Date	Type	Frequency

PESTS

Date	Type	Treatment

DISEASES

Date	Type	Treatment

Plant Compendium

COMMON NAME

_____

LATIN NAME

_____

DESCRIPTION

_____

_____

_____

_____

_____

_____

Draw the plant, paste a picture, or paste a leaf press.

MAGICAL PROPERTIES

_____

_____

_____

_____

MAGICAL CORRESPONDENCES/FOLKLORE

_____

_____

_____

_____

MAGICAL NOTES Record spells or charms you used; magical elements that visited the garden.

PLANTING HISTORY

Task	Date	Notes
Started seeds:		
Germination:		
Transplanted:		
Bloom date:		
Harvest date:		

CULTURE NOTES Make notes about the ideal conditions for this plant.

USDA zone	3A/B	4A/B	5A/B	6A/B	7A/B	8A/B	9A/B	10A/B
Soil type	Sandy	Loamy	Clay	Mixed	Potting mix			
Water needs	Low	Medium	High	Aquatic	Air			
Sunlight	Shade	Moderate	Full sun	Direct	Indirect			

FERTILIZER SCHEDULE

Date	Type	Frequency

PRUNING/TRIMMING SCHEDULE

Date	Type	Frequency

PESTS

Date	Type	Treatment

DISEASES

Date	Type	Treatment

 # Plant Compendium

COMMON NAME

_____

LATIN NAME

_____

DESCRIPTION

_____

_____

_____

_____

_____

_____

Draw the plant, paste a picture, or paste a leaf press.

MAGICAL PROPERTIES

_____

_____

_____

_____

MAGICAL CORRESPONDENCES/FOLKLORE

_____

_____

_____

_____

MAGICAL NOTES Record spells or charms you used; magical elements that visited the garden.

PLANTING HISTORY

Task	Date	Notes
Started seeds:		
Germination:		
Transplanted:		
Bloom date:		
Harvest date:		

CULTURE NOTES Make notes about the ideal conditions for this plant.

USDA zone	3A/B	4A/B	5A/B	6A/B	7A/B	8A/B	9A/B	10A/B
Soil type	Sandy	Loamy	Clay	Mixed	Potting mix
Water needs	Low	Medium	High	Aquatic	Air
Sunlight	Shade	Moderate	Full sun	Direct	Indirect

FERTILIZER SCHEDULE

Date	Type	Frequency

PRUNING/TRIMMING SCHEDULE

Date	Type	Frequency

PESTS

Date	Type	Treatment

DISEASES

Date	Type	Treatment

Plant Compendium

COMMON NAME

_____

LATIN NAME

_____

DESCRIPTION

_____

_____

_____

_____

_____

_____

Draw the plant, paste a picture, or paste a leaf press.

MAGICAL PROPERTIES

_____

_____

_____

_____

MAGICAL CORRESPONDENCES/FOLKLORE

_____

_____

_____

_____

MAGICAL NOTES Record spells or charms you used; magical elements that visited the garden.

PLANTING HISTORY

Task	Date	Notes
Started seeds:		
Germination:		
Transplanted:		
Bloom date:		
Harvest date:		

CULTURE NOTES Make notes about the ideal conditions for this plant.

USDA zone	3A/B	4A/B	5A/B	6A/B	7A/B	8A/B	9A/B	10A/B
Soil type	Sandy	Loamy	Clay	Mixed	Potting mix			
Water needs	Low	Medium	High	Aquatic	Air			
Sunlight	Shade	Moderate	Full sun	Direct	Indirect			

FERTILIZER SCHEDULE

Date	*Type*	*Frequency*

PRUNING/TRIMMING SCHEDULE

Date	*Type*	*Frequency*

PESTS

Date	*Type*	*Treatment*

DISEASES

Date	*Type*	*Treatment*

Plant Compendium

COMMON NAME

_____

LATIN NAME

_____

DESCRIPTION

_____

_____

_____

_____

_____

_____

Draw the plant, paste a picture, or paste a leaf press.

MAGICAL PROPERTIES

_____

_____

_____

MAGICAL CORRESPONDENCES/FOLKLORE

_____

_____

_____

_____

MAGICAL NOTES Record spells or charms you used; magical elements that visited the garden.

PLANTING HISTORY

Task	Date	Notes
Started seeds:		
Germination:		
Transplanted:		
Bloom date:		
Harvest date:		

CULTURE NOTES Make notes about the ideal conditions for this plant.

USDA zone	3A/B	4A/B	5A/B	6A/B	7A/B	8A/B	9A/B	10A/B
Soil type	Sandy	Loamy		Clay		Mixed		Potting mix
Water needs	Low	Medium		High		Aquatic		Air
Sunlight	Shade	Moderate		Full sun		Direct		Indirect

FERTILIZER SCHEDULE

Date	Type	Frequency

PRUNING/TRIMMING SCHEDULE

Date	Type	Frequency

PESTS

Date	Type	Treatment

DISEASES

Date	Type	Treatment

Plant Compendium

COMMON NAME

_____

LATIN NAME

_____

DESCRIPTION

_____

_____

_____

_____

_____

_____

Draw the plant, paste a picture, or paste a leaf press.

MAGICAL PROPERTIES

_____

_____

_____

_____

MAGICAL CORRESPONDENCES/FOLKLORE

_____

_____

_____

_____

MAGICAL NOTES Record spells or charms you used; magical elements that visited the garden.

PLANTING HISTORY

Task	Date	Notes
Started seeds:		
Germination:		
Transplanted:		
Bloom date:		
Harvest date:		

CULTURE NOTES   Make notes about the ideal conditions for this plant.

USDA zone	3A/B	4A/B	5A/B	6A/B	7A/B	8A/B	9A/B	10A/B
Soil type	Sandy	Loamy	Clay	Mixed	Potting mix			
Water needs	Low	Medium	High	Aquatic	Air			
Sunlight	Shade	Moderate	Full sun	Direct	Indirect			

FERTILIZER SCHEDULE

Date	Type	Frequency

PRUNING/TRIMMING SCHEDULE

Date	Type	Frequency

PESTS

Date	Type	Treatment

DISEASES

Date	Type	Treatment

Plant Compendium

COMMON NAME

_____

LATIN NAME

_____

DESCRIPTION

_____
_____
_____
_____
_____
_____

Draw the plant, paste a picture, or paste a leaf press.

MAGICAL PROPERTIES

_____
_____
_____
_____

MAGICAL CORRESPONDENCES/FOLKLORE

_____
_____
_____
_____

MAGICAL NOTES Record spells or charms you used; magical elements that visited the garden.

PLANTING HISTORY

Task	Date	Notes
Started seeds:		
Germination:		
Transplanted:		
Bloom date:		
Harvest date:		

CULTURE NOTES Make notes about the ideal conditions for this plant.

USDA zone	3A/B	4A/B	5A/B	6A/B	7A/B	8A/B	9A/B	10A/B
Soil type	Sandy	Loamy	Clay		Mixed	Potting mix		
Water needs	Low	Medium	High		Aquatic	Air		
Sunlight	Shade	Moderate	Full sun		Direct	Indirect		

FERTILIZER SCHEDULE

Date	*Type*	*Frequency*

PRUNING/TRIMMING SCHEDULE

Date	*Type*	*Frequency*

PESTS

Date	*Type*	*Treatment*

DISEASES

Date	*Type*	*Treatment*

 # *Plant Compendium*

COMMON NAME

_____

LATIN NAME

_____

DESCRIPTION

_____

_____

_____

_____

_____

_____

MAGICAL PROPERTIES   **MAGICAL CORRESPONDENCES/FOLKLORE**

_____   _____

_____   _____

_____   _____

_____   _____

MAGICAL NOTES Record spells or charms you used; magical elements that visited the garden.

PLANTING HISTORY

Task	Date	Notes
Started seeds:		
Germination:		
Transplanted:		
Bloom date:		
Harvest date:		

CULTURE NOTES Make notes about the ideal conditions for this plant.

USDA zone	3A/B	4A/B	5A/B	6A/B	7A/B	8A/B	9A/B	10A/B
Soil type	Sandy	Loamy	Clay	Mixed	Potting mix
Water needs	Low	Medium	High	Aquatic	Air
Sunlight	Shade	Moderate	Full sun	Direct	Indirect

FERTILIZER SCHEDULE

Date	Type	Frequency

PRUNING/TRIMMING SCHEDULE

Date	Type	Frequency

PESTS

Date	Type	Treatment

DISEASES

Date	Type	Treatment

 # Plant Compendium

COMMON NAME

_____

LATIN NAME

_____

DESCRIPTION

_____

_____

_____

_____

_____

_____

MAGICAL PROPERTIES

_____

_____

_____

_____

MAGICAL CORRESPONDENCES/FOLKLORE

_____

_____

_____

_____

MAGICAL NOTES   Record spells or charms you used; magical elements that visited the garden.

PLANTING HISTORY

Task	Date	Notes
Started seeds:		
Germination:		
Transplanted:		
Bloom date:		
Harvest date:		

CULTURE NOTES Make notes about the ideal conditions for this plant.

USDA zone	3A/B	4A/B	5A/B	6A/B	7A/B	8A/B	9A/B	10A/B
Soil type	Sandy	Loamy	Clay	Mixed	Potting mix
Water needs	Low	Medium	High	Aquatic	Air
Sunlight	Shade	Moderate	Full sun	Direct	Indirect

FERTILIZER SCHEDULE

Date	Type	Frequency

PRUNING/TRIMMING SCHEDULE

Date	Type	Frequency

PESTS

Date	Type	Treatment

DISEASES

Date	Type	Treatment

 # Plant Compendium

COMMON NAME

_____

LATIN NAME

_____

DESCRIPTION

_____

_____

_____

_____

_____

_____

Draw the plant, paste a picture, or paste a leaf press.

MAGICAL PROPERTIES   **MAGICAL CORRESPONDENCES/FOLKLORE**

_____   _____

_____   _____

_____   _____

_____   _____

MAGICAL NOTES Record spells or charms you used; magical elements that visited the garden.

PLANTING HISTORY

Task	Date	Notes
Started seeds:		
Germination:		
Transplanted:		
Bloom date:		
Harvest date:		

CULTURE NOTES Make notes about the ideal conditions for this plant.

USDA zone	3A/B	4A/B	5A/B	6A/B	7A/B	8A/B	9A/B	10A/B
Soil type	Sandy	Loamy	Clay	Mixed	Potting mix
Water needs	Low	Medium	High	Aquatic	Air
Sunlight	Shade	Moderate	Full sun	Direct	Indirect

FERTILIZER SCHEDULE

Date	Type	Frequency

PRUNING/TRIMMING SCHEDULE

Date	Type	Frequency

PESTS

Date	Type	Treatment

DISEASES

Date	Type	Treatment

COMMON NAME

_____

LATIN NAME

_____

DESCRIPTION

_____

_____

_____

_____

_____

_____

Draw the plant, paste a picture, or paste a leaf press.

MAGICAL PROPERTIES

_____

_____

_____

_____

MAGICAL CORRESPONDENCES/FOLKLORE

_____

_____

_____

_____

MAGICAL NOTES   Record spells or charms you used; magical elements that visited the garden.

PLANTING HISTORY

Task	Date	Notes
Started seeds:		
Germination:		
Transplanted:		
Bloom date:		
Harvest date:		

CULTURE NOTES Make notes about the ideal conditions for this plant.

USDA zone	3A/B	4A/B	5A/B	6A/B	7A/B	8A/B	9A/B	10A/B
Soil type	Sandy	Loamy	Clay		Mixed		Potting mix	
Water needs	Low	Medium	High		Aquatic	Air		
Sunlight	Shade	Moderate	Full sun		Direct	Indirect		

FERTILIZER SCHEDULE

Date	Type	Frequency

PRUNING/TRIMMING SCHEDULE

Date	Type	Frequency

PESTS

Date	Type	Treatment

DISEASES

Date	Type	Treatment

Plant Compendium

COMMON NAME

_____

LATIN NAME

_____

DESCRIPTION

_____

_____

_____

_____

_____

Draw the plant, paste a picture, or paste a leaf press.

MAGICAL PROPERTIES

_____

_____

_____

_____

MAGICAL CORRESPONDENCES/FOLKLORE

_____

_____

_____

_____

MAGICAL NOTES Record spells or charms you used; magical elements that visited the garden.

218

PLANTING HISTORY

Task	Date	Notes
Started seeds:		
Germination:		
Transplanted:		
Bloom date:		
Harvest date:		

CULTURE NOTES Make notes about the ideal conditions for this plant.

USDA zone	3A/B	4A/B	5A/B	6A/B	7A/B	8A/B	9A/B	10A/B
Soil type	Sandy	Loamy		Clay		Mixed	Potting mix	
Water needs	Low	Medium		High		Aquatic	Air	
Sunlight	Shade	Moderate		Full sun		Direct	Indirect	

FERTILIZER SCHEDULE

Date	*Type*	*Frequency*

PRUNING/TRIMMING SCHEDULE

Date	*Type*	*Frequency*

PESTS

Date	*Type*	*Treatment*

DISEASES

Date	*Type*	*Treatment*

Plant Compendium

COMMON NAME

_____

LATIN NAME

_____

DESCRIPTION

_____
_____
_____
_____
_____
_____

Draw the plant, paste a picture, or paste a leaf press.

MAGICAL PROPERTIES

_____
_____
_____
_____

MAGICAL CORRESPONDENCES/FOLKLORE

_____
_____
_____
_____

MAGICAL NOTES   Record spells or charms you used; magical elements that visited the garden.

PLANTING HISTORY

Task	Date	Notes
Started seeds:		
Germination:		
Transplanted:		
Bloom date:		
Harvest date:		

CULTURE NOTES Make notes about the ideal conditions for this plant.

USDA zone	3A/B	4A/B	5A/B	6A/B	7A/B	8A/B	9A/B	10A/B

Soil type   Sandy   Loamy   Clay   Mixed   Potting mix

Water needs   Low   Medium   High   Aquatic   Air

Sunlight   Shade   Moderate   Full sun   Direct   Indirect

FERTILIZER SCHEDULE

Date	*Type*	*Frequency*

PRUNING/TRIMMING SCHEDULE

Date	*Type*	*Frequency*

PESTS

Date	*Type*	*Treatment*

DISEASES

Date	*Type*	*Treatment*

Plant Compendium

COMMON NAME

_____

LATIN NAME

_____

DESCRIPTION

_____

_____

_____

_____

_____

MAGICAL PROPERTIES

_____

_____

_____

_____

MAGICAL CORRESPONDENCES/FOLKLORE

_____

_____

_____

_____

MAGICAL NOTES Record spells or charms you used; magical elements that visited the garden.

PLANTING HISTORY

Task	Date	Notes
Started seeds:		
Germination:		
Transplanted:		
Bloom date:		
Harvest date:		

CULTURE NOTES Make notes about the ideal conditions for this plant.

USDA zone	3A/B	4A/B	5A/B	6A/B	7A/B	8A/B	9A/B	10A/B
Soil type	Sandy	Loamy		Clay		Mixed		Potting mix
Water needs	Low	Medium		High		Aquatic	Air	
Sunlight	Shade	Moderate		Full sun		Direct	Indirect	

FERTILIZER SCHEDULE

Date	Type	Frequency

PRUNING/TRIMMING SCHEDULE

Date	Type	Frequency

PESTS

Date	Type	Treatment

DISEASES

Date	Type	Treatment

Plant Compendium

COMMON NAME

LATIN NAME

DESCRIPTION

MAGICAL PROPERTIES   **MAGICAL CORRESPONDENCES/FOLKLORE**

MAGICAL NOTES Record spells or charms you used; magical elements that visited the garden.

PLANTING HISTORY

Task	Date	Notes
Started seeds:		
Germination:		
Transplanted:		
Bloom date:		
Harvest date:		

CULTURE NOTES Make notes about the ideal conditions for this plant.

USDA zone	3A/B	4A/B	5A/B	6A/B	7A/B	8A/B	9A/B	10A/B
Soil type	Sandy	Loamy	Clay	Mixed	Potting mix
Water needs	Low	Medium	High	Aquatic	Air
Sunlight	Shade	Moderate	Full sun	Direct	Indirect

FERTILIZER SCHEDULE

Date	Type	Frequency

PRUNING/TRIMMING SCHEDULE

Date	Type	Frequency

PESTS

Date	Type	Treatment

DISEASES

Date	Type	Treatment

 # Plant Compendium

COMMON NAME

_____

LATIN NAME

_____

DESCRIPTION

_____

_____

_____

_____

_____

_____

Draw the plant, paste a picture, or paste a leaf press.

MAGICAL PROPERTIES

_____

_____

_____

_____

MAGICAL CORRESPONDENCES/FOLKLORE

_____

_____

_____

_____

MAGICAL NOTES   Record spells or charms you used; magical elements that visited the garden.

PLANTING HISTORY

Task	Date	Notes
Started seeds:		
Germination:		
Transplanted:		
Bloom date:		
Harvest date:		

CULTURE NOTES Make notes about the ideal conditions for this plant.

USDA zone	3A/B	4A/B	5A/B	6A/B	7A/B	8A/B	9A/B	10A/B
Soil type	Sandy	Loamy	Clay	Mixed	Potting mix			
Water needs	Low	Medium	High	Aquatic	Air			
Sunlight	Shade	Moderate	Full sun	Direct	Indirect			

FERTILIZER SCHEDULE

Date	Type	Frequency

PRUNING/TRIMMING SCHEDULE

Date	Type	Frequency

PESTS

Date	Type	Treatment

DISEASES

Date	Type	Treatment

 # Plant Compendium

COMMON NAME

_____

LATIN NAME

_____

DESCRIPTION

_____

_____

_____

_____

_____

_____

MAGICAL PROPERTIES

_____

_____

_____

_____

MAGICAL CORRESPONDENCES/FOLKLORE

_____

_____

_____

_____

MAGICAL NOTES Record spells or charms you used; magical elements that visited the garden.

PLANTING HISTORY

Task	Date	Notes
Started seeds:		
Germination:		
Transplanted:		
Bloom date:		
Harvest date:		

CULTURE NOTES Make notes about the ideal conditions for this plant.

USDA zone	3A/B	4A/B	5A/B	6A/B	7A/B	8A/B	9A/B 10A/B
Soil type	Sandy	Loamy	Clay	Mixed	Potting mix		
Water needs	Low	Medium	High	Aquatic	Air		
Sunlight	Shade	Moderate	Full sun	Direct	Indirect		

FERTILIZER SCHEDULE

Date	Type	Frequency

PRUNING/TRIMMING SCHEDULE

Date	Type	Frequency

PESTS

Date	Type	Treatment

DISEASES

Date	Type	Treatment

Plant Compendium

COMMON NAME

LATIN NAME

DESCRIPTION

Draw the plant, paste a picture, or paste a leaf press.

MAGICAL PROPERTIES

MAGICAL CORRESPONDENCES/FOLKLORE

MAGICAL NOTES Record spells or charms you used; magical elements that visited the garden.

PLANTING HISTORY

Task	Date	Notes
Started seeds:		
Germination:		
Transplanted:		
Bloom date:		
Harvest date:		

CULTURE NOTES Make notes about the ideal conditions for this plant.

USDA zone	3A/B	4A/B	5A/B	6A/B	7A/B	8A/B	9A/B	10A/B
Soil type	Sandy	Loamy		Clay		Mixed		Potting mix
Water needs	Low	Medium		High		Aquatic		Air
Sunlight	Shade	Moderate		Full sun		Direct		Indirect

FERTILIZER SCHEDULE

Date	*Type*	*Frequency*

PRUNING/TRIMMING SCHEDULE

Date	*Type*	*Frequency*

PESTS

Date	*Type*	*Treatment*

DISEASES

Date	*Type*	*Treatment*

 # Plant Compendium

COMMON NAME

_____

LATIN NAME

_____

DESCRIPTION

_____

_____

_____

_____

_____

_____

Draw the plant, paste a picture, or paste a leaf press.

MAGICAL PROPERTIES

_____

_____

_____

_____

MAGICAL CORRESPONDENCES/FOLKLORE

_____

_____

_____

_____

MAGICAL NOTES Record spells or charms you used; magical elements that visited the garden.

PLANTING HISTORY

Task	Date	Notes
Started seeds:		
Germination:		
Transplanted:		
Bloom date:		
Harvest date:		

CULTURE NOTES   Make notes about the ideal conditions for this plant.

USDA zone	3A/B	4A/B	5A/B	6A/B	7A/B	8A/B	9A/B	10A/B
Soil type	Sandy	Loamy		Clay		Mixed	Potting mix	
Water needs	Low	Medium		High		Aquatic	Air	
Sunlight	Shade	Moderate		Full sun		Direct	Indirect	

FERTILIZER SCHEDULE

Date	Type	Frequency

PRUNING/TRIMMING SCHEDULE

Date	Type	Frequency

PESTS

Date	Type	Treatment

DISEASES

Date	Type	Treatment

Index

COMPLETE YOUR
GREEN WITCH
LIBRARY TODAY

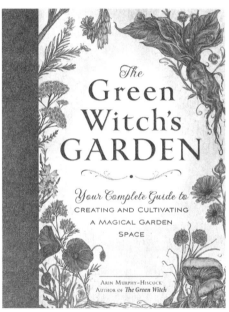

PICK UP OR DOWNLOAD
YOUR COPIES TODAY!